TRIAL BY MEDIA

China's new show trials,

and the global expansion of Chinese media

ISBN: 978-0-9993706-2-9

First edition.

Keywords: Forced TV Confessions, China, Media
Human Rights, Criminal Justice

Also available as Kindle book:

ISBN: 978-0-9993706-6-7

https://SafeguardDefenders.com

ALSO BY SAFEGUARS DEFENDERS

The People's Republic of the Disappeared, the first book on the subject of China's use of Enforced Disappearances through the legalized system euphemistically named Residential Surveillance at a Designated Location (RSDL), exposes the systematic use of secret imprisonment and torture of lawyers, media workers, and government critics.

The book, released to widespread praise for its powerful victim testimonies and lucid legal analysis, is available in English as both paperback and Kindle editions through Amazon worldwide (ISBN 978-0999370605). The **Chinese edition** (ISBN 978-1981289820) is also available as a paperback.

Scripted and Staged: Behind the scenes of China's forced televised confessions is a groundbreaking publication that gives the reader a backstage pass to China's production and broadcast of coerced confessions by human rights lawyers, journalists, activists, and foreigners. This is the report that laid the ground for *Trial by Media*, the book you are now holding in your hand.

Using in-depth interviews and analysis of hours of broadcast confessions, **Scripted and Staged** exposes how the Chinese state uses threats and torture to force victims into confessing, how China's media collaborate in their recording, production, and broadcast across the globe. The publication is available as a paperback on Amazon worldwide (ISBN 978-1983743375) and for free download at RSDLmonitor.com.

TABLE OF CONTENTS

A note on "709 crackdown" and "RSDL"

709, or the 709 crackdown, draws its name from the date it started. On the evening of June 9 (2015), one of China's most prominent civil rights lawyers, Wang Yu, had her home raided and was taken away. Later that night, her husband, Bao Longjun, who had taken their son to the Beijing airport to see him off as he was set to go study in Australia, was apprehended and taken away. Their son was placed in house arrest in faraway Inner Mongolia. The next day, many other lawyers, all over China, started disappearing. The last key target, lawyer Wang Quanzhang, was taken in early August after evading police. By that time, hundreds of lawyers had been taken, some for short-term detention, some would disappear. Wang Quanzhang remains missing, three years later.

These lawyers and legal activists were all part of the "rights defense" community, a small group that had gained renown for pushing for rule of law and human rights protections using China's own laws. With this, they had themselves become the main target. The 709 crackdown, sometimes referred to as the "war on law" and "war on lawyers" continue to play out, three years later.

The crackdown exposed several new trends in how the CCP chooses to persecute, from the use of RSDL, to the use of forced TV confessions, to "non-release release" and attacks on family members and loved ones, using a scorched earth tactic.

RSDL, or "residential surveillance at a designated location" is a new tool, allowing police to take anyone, and hold them for six months in solitary confinement and incommunicado. It's a system for enforced disappearances, and while inside, people are meant to disappear. For that purpose, the police may not use detention centers or prisons. Instead, converted rooms in government-run guesthouses and special custom-built secret prisons are used. Inside, not even the prosecutor can visit you to make sure you are not tortured.

Likewise, it was with the rampant use of forcing these lawyers to make televised confessions, always before trial, that this new phenomenon under Xi Jinping has become well-known.

For those not sentenced to long-term imprisonment, like lawyer Zhou Shifeng who was sentenced to seven years, many others instead spent between one and two years, first in RSDL and later in pre-trial detention, only to be released on bail, or in "non-release release" after having been paraded, sometimes numerous times, on TV. "Non-release release" was coined as a term by noted law scholar Jerome Cohen, after witnessing how the state would announce someone released, only for them to disappear. Only many months later would they emerge, often having been illegally held under house arrest away from their families.

This book will also show a final, new, trends, namely how the state is now not only attacking the "suspect", but will seek to destroy the "suspects" family. Local government can demolish their houses while they are kept locked up, the police seek out to destroy their families businesses and livelihood, refuse their kids access to schooling, or even beat up and detain their kids, siblings or loved ones. This new mode of persecution, the *scorched earth model*, shows the tenacity and courage of these rights defenders, and police seem to have realized that mere imprisonment and torture of the "suspect" is many times not enough to discourage them from continuing their work.

The testimonies in this book will show all these trends, and how it relates to their forced televised confessions, their trials by media.

TRIAL BY MEDIA
China's new show trials, and the global expansion of Chinese media

Chapter 1

Introduction | **PETER DAHLIN**

On a Friday, February 9, 2018, an unhealthy looking Swedish citizen greeted cameras, sitting, surrounded by police officers, in a detention center, ostentatiously answering questions from journalists from Chinese media, debasing himself and criticizing others, including the foreign government which was trying to help him. That man was not me, although I had experienced something similar myself not long before. This was another Swede, the author and publisher Gui Minhai.

The twists and turns of his story have made headlines since he mysteriously vanished in 2015. Gui Minhai was one of five booksellers from Hong Kong, each who disappeared, one by one reappearing under questionable circumstances in China. Unlike the others, however, he didn't disappear from Hong Kong, but was kidnapped in Thailand. Before that Friday in February, he had already been made to appear confessing to crimes or denouncing others on TV twice. His experience was too extreme not to become a major story, big enough to also highlight the otherwise little analyzed phenomenon that's become more popular in China since the rise of Xi Jinping – the use of Forced TV Confessions.

Forcing people to confess on TV isn't itself anything new in China, but the increase in its use, designed not only for domestic propaganda but for global reach, and to shape foreign policy, require us to take a deeper look. With foreign targets and victims, the use of torture, drugging and threats to loved ones, with the aim of coercing confessions to crimes for which victims are often never brought to trial, have shown how precarious China's judicial system is, and how little trust can be placed in the system. After all, most confessions are extracted not merely before prosecution, but even before arrest.

A changing China

During Xi Jinping's first five years in power, China has witnessed a massive overhaul of its legal system and a restructuring of the state itself - both processes aimed at giving the state, the Chinese Communist Party, and, ultimately, Xi Jinping himself, more power.

First, a new system for investigation and detention, euphemistically called "residential surveillance at a designated location" (RSDL), allowing police to hold suspects for six months, without court approval, and without having to notify anyone of the person's whereabouts, has been put in place. It denies the suspect the right to a lawyer, and keeps the detained outside of prisons and detention centers, whether in reconfigured hotel rooms, police training facilities, army barracks or custom-built secret prisons. Even the prosecutors, who in China work side by side with the police, are denied access. Most of the known victims has been lawyers, journalists, NGO workers or those related to underground house churches.

Secondly, the party itself has ramped up its internal "disciplinary investigations" into China's 85 million party members, and the extensive use of "Shuanggui", a system similar to RSDL allowing for near-endless detention of suspects, without any legal safeguards at all, has continued unabated. In 2016 the CCP moved to expand this system, moving it beyond merely the party and its members. By 2018, the constitution was revised, establishing the *National Supervision Commission* (NSC). Corruption is supposedly the main target, but in reality it concerns any actions deemed politically incorrect. It has its own investigation and detention system, completely outside the judicial system. It is not limited to CCP members, but all state workers, managers working for public institutions, hospitals, schools and state-owned enterprises, and others on public payroll, like contractors, or for that matter, anyone somehow related to a breach in discipline or corruption, say, a family member, a child or a foreign businessman. Once investigated under this system, the NSC can, like police within RSDL, hold the person for six months at secret locations with no legal safeguards.

With these developments, China has carved away a significant part of what would otherwise fall under the authority of the judicial system, already subservient to the party, and placed exceeding power directly in the hands of the party. At the same time, the judicial system itself has been significantly weakened, with new laws concerning "national security" and "terrorism" stripping away many of the rights otherwise afforded suspects.

Together, over a period of some five years, two developments concerning the legal system appeared. One is the further watering down of already weak or nonexistent protections of those suspected of crimes (and handled within the normal judicial system), and two is the establishment of systems for investigation and detention outside the judicial system. In effect, new systems have been established to limit the jurisdiction of the judicial system, in which even limited procedural safeguards are abandoned.

It is within these dual attacks on the already limited and broken legal system, that the phenomena of Forced TV Confessions should be viewed. Its use plays a crucial role for the Party, and puts another nail in the coffin on the idea of any system of governing China according to the rule of law.

TRIAL BY MEDIA
China's new show trials, and the global expansion of Chinese media

That China has further abandoned international human rights norms and embraced forced TV confessions as a matter of policy, with an increasingly international target audience, has certainly come to light since my own televised forced confession, and been emphasized again and again each time Gui Minhai has been paraded in front of the cameras. But it wasn't truly until the Safeguard Defenders report *Scripted and Staged*, which is the basis for this book, until much of the international media and others began to report on the expanded use of forced television confessions as part of a system and not as individual episodes.

The same report would also go on to expose the actual process of how these televised confessions work, what goes on behind the scenes, how the Chinese state media plays an active role as collaborators, and how many of these confessions are not for mere internal propaganda, but also active tools of foreign policy.

Gui's last "confession" was a case in point – his answers, in reality a clearly prepared statement read with little regard to the questions asked by the journalists read more or less like a statement coming from the spokesperson for the Chinese Foreign Ministry targeting Sweden. Or take these short statements, widely panned by his daughter as sounding nothing like how he would ever speak:

> *"Looking back, I might have become Sweden's chess piece. I broke the law again under their instigation. My wonderful life has been ruined and I would never trust the Swedish ever again."*

> *"The year 2018 is election year in Sweden ... some politicians might be using me for political gains. I can't*

*rule out that some are trying to use me to create trouble
for the Chinese government."*

Anyone familiar with the prepared remarks of the Chinese Foreign Ministry will feel a sense of déjà vu.

His last confession was a collaboration between Chinese police, the Foreign Ministry, the CCP and select Chinese media, alongside Hong Kong's South China Morning Post. Together, they made his confession. Gui himself was almost irrelevant in a sense, sitting there like a teleprompter reading what he had been told to read, showing an expression he without doubt had been told to show.

Foreign media and failure to report

The foreign media's response to the new Gui Minhai "confession" in itself contributed to the need to expose the reality behind these TV "confessions". The report *Scripted and Staged* had at this point already been in the making for some time. Collecting data on such a large number of televised confessions, analyzing them to find patterns, and more than anything, getting victims to speak in public for the first time, was a daunting task.

One lawyer, Zhang Kai, once released, posted on his social media that he had been forced to say what he said. After exposing that his confession had been forced, he was taken by police again mere days after. Zhai Yanmin posted an apology on social media soon after his release, after having given three televised confessions. Police didn't take long to visit him, telling him to remove the post immediately and to never think of doing something like that again.

The risk of speaking out is very real, even for those who choose to only speak using pseudonyms. But many of them did speak out nevertheless, and from the stories they wrote for us, and the interviews conducted with others, many patterns became clear. Releasing the report has helped the world's media understand the reality behind it all, and for them to better report on such televised confessions in the future. Likewise, in all those televised confessions where foreigners were the victim, or the person was accused of anything with a foreign connection, it became key to make governments and diplomats understand how these are used as tools of foreign policy.

After the report's release, and the extensive coverage that followed, in radio, TV, print and online, a little less than two weeks later, two Canadians were paraded on TV while in police custody, incriminating themselves and attacking others, with foreign media yet again failing to cover their "confessions" and the larger issue at hand in a way that takes into account journalistic ethics and the reality of the issue.

It's not hard to understand why. Even those publications with the most far-reaching China coverage, and with reporters who in my view rank as some of the best covering China, media's work has become even harder in China, with a deteriorating situation since Xi Jinping came to power. On top of that, the sensational aspect of each new Forced TV Confession would make it hard to resist instant coverage. Unfortunately, such coverage often plays right into the hands of the CCP, giving them exactly what they want. Exposing the truth behind these "confessions", and the system behind it, will be key for foreign media in future coverage.

The "confessions"

The "confession" usually takes place whilst the suspect is in detention – not after arrest, certainly not after prosecution. It takes place without the suspect having had a chance to consult with any lawyer, in fact, access to a lawyer before prosecution is becoming rarer and rarer in China– another side of China's quickly weakening legal system.

As such, the "confession" made and broadcast sets the frame of any following legal process – from arrest, to prosecution, to trial and sentencing. At the same time, it allows the state to use it for propaganda, or in some cases, as instruments of foreign policy. Because a confession is already extracted, the legal process that follows becomes meaningless.

As the brief testimonies in *Scripted and Staged* showed, and how the stories in this book shows, extensive physical and mental torture is not only common, but almost guaranteed. Drugging of victims has been noted in several cases, with pills forced upon the victims, often with significant psychological effects. If anything stands out in reading these testimonials, it's the fact that torture – physical and mental – seems not enough to break many of them, seems not enough to make them do these televised confessions, and in the end police need to resort to detaining, threatening to detain, or beating and torturing the victims' spouses or children to get them to the point where they say yes.

I myself, as a foreigner, was treated better during my time in RSDL than most victims. Nonetheless, the police wanted what they wanted, and were willing to take the steps to get it, or take "measures" as the police called it when threatening Liu Sixin. Whether to make such a recording or not wasn't merely a matter of if I wanted to improve my chances of release, but if I wanted my Chinese girlfriend released – she was sitting in solitary confinement every day that I was, and would continue to do so for up to six months, unless I worked with them to find a "solution", i.e., agreeing to deliver the confession they wanted to hear.

As Zhai Yanmin writes:

> *"They cuffed my hands behind my back, they locked me to iron railings, they would use five or six electric batons to beat me. For a long period they didn't let me eat, or drink water, or go to the bathroom. They subjected me to so many kinds of torture. Yet, it was nothing compared with their threats that they would detain my son."*

It's not always enough to merely threaten the children of the suspects, sometimes going so far as to detain them, to keep them as pawns to be played against the suspect. Or in the case of Wang Yu's teenage son, they detained him, beat him, and forced him to write down allegations against others. As Wang Yu recalls, long after her own release.

> *"They made my son frame other people. They told him exactly what he had to say. He didn't agree, so they hit him, with a thick, long wooden staff. They started at him in the lower back, moving higher and higher, smashing it into his back, while yelling: "If you don't write what we say, we're going to go all the way up to your head and smash your skull in."*

The legal system does not allow for any meaningful way to have the confession thrown out at trial because it was extracted through torture. And in some cases, the things confessed to will change from the actual TV confession to any confession given later at, say, a trial. Sometimes the change in their confession, or even the crime they are accused of, changes so much it is ludicrous.

The broadcast of the confessions undermines the limited rule of law China claims to have adopted. It directly deprives the victim of the constitutionally guaranteed right to a fair trial. It's not often judicial officers speak out against party rule in China, but once the use of these televised confessions became clear, Zhu Zhengfu, vice-chair of the All-China Lawyers Association, felt compelled to issue a public criticism against the use of these confessions[1].

The broadcasts themselves, as the stories in this book and in *Scripted and Staged* – the findings of which are summarized in Chapter 10, shows, are scripted, staged and directed to appear a certain way. Like any theatre production, the phenomenon begins with a script written, only one that the victim has little sway over.

The producers arrange the setting, whether inside the victim's detention center, or in a hotel suite, in the CCTV headquarters in Beijing, or in some garden setting. Clothes are decided on, be it civilian clothing handed to them, their own clothing from when they were detained, or the use of prison garments. All of it depending on what role the victim's TV confession is supposed to serve.

The actual recording, whether by the victim and police, or in some cases agents from the Ministry of State Security, or by the victim and journalists brought in, remains the same: actors, acting out a script based on questions and answers. The victim is given time to memorize the script, but if needed, large cue cards will be arranged to be held in front of the victim, to help them get it right.

The director, often the main investigator of the victim's case will handle decisions on re-takes, of which there are often many. Tone, expression, posture, speed of voice, all need be considered.

When media is involved, production values tend to be higher, and with media involvement, the amount of post-production work tends to be more extensive. However, even for those recordings made by police alone, there is often extensive post-production added before its broadcast on CCTV or other TV channels. A day of recordings will often end up as maybe one minute of actual "interview" or "confession", baked into longer segments.

And if there is any mistake at this point, let it be clear - the journalist will act his or her role as an actor, just like the victim. Most times they will have the same paper, and the journalist will simply read the questions. In some, the media is simply there to observe and record, and the police will read the questions directly. The role of the journalist ranges from minor to major. Liu Sixin's writing shows clearly how a journalist did more than merely ask the questions:

> *"Wang Yu arrived, let's finish here. We can do it again if needed"* - This is CCTV journalist Dong Qian, in response to hearing that lawyer Wang Yu had arrived, directing other journalists and police while extracting a "confession" from Professor Liu Sixin.

The stories you will read in this book range from those scripted, recorded and produced by the police themselves and then merely broadcast by CCTV or other media, to those made and produced in active collaboration with the media. Likewise, you will read about how recordings are made in different settings – from detention centers and secret prisons, often showing the person in a custodial setting, to those produced in alternative settings – grand hotel suites, a garden, a mock courtroom, where the person wears civilian clothing. Forced TV Confessions are not static, and over time, as chapter 10 will show, you can notice significant changes in the forms they take. By slowly changing the form of these televised "confessions", it is most certainly the aim of the CCP and police to disorient the media that reports on them – to keep these effective it cannot be too obvious that they are indeed Forced TV Confessions. The eight short stories, along with analysis of trends over the last five years of televised confessions, seeks to make clear what these are, how they are made, and how people are treated to place them in a situation where they cannot say no.

Confessions, self-criticisms and show trials

The systematic use of Forced TV Confessions did not come out of thin air, and it's often noted that it reminds people of the use of public self-criticisms in the past. Though little research has been done so far into the use of Forced TV Confessions, it is in fact another Swede, Magnus Fiskesjö, indeed a former cultural attaché at the Swedish Embassy in Beijing (1985-1988), and now a Professor at Cornell University in the U.S., who has researched the background of these more modern, televised, forms of self-criticisms.

Whereas such public self-criticisms before were primarily a tool of the CCP, a tool for power struggles within the party, or a tool for domestic propaganda by the party, it has now been incorporated into the state and judicial system. He notes that China's use of these televised confessions represents a modern take on the show trials of Stalin's Soviet Union[2], an observation that becomes even clearer in chapter 2, where Zhai Yanmin first describes the endless recordings for his televised confession – long before he was ever arrested, but then details how he, the police, judge and prosecutor together worked, using the very same methods, to prepare him for his actual trial, including a mock trial for practice. Only, as he notes, for the trial there was no room for retakes.

Professor Fiskesjö goes further, in a study entitled *The Return of the Show Trial: China's Televised "Confessions*[3] to note that these kinds of TV confessions "...are closely related to one key element in this authoritarian turn — to go beyond the mere silencing of alternative voices and opinions, and "shape reality."" This aspect is made clear by the fact, as *Scripted and Staged* notes, as well as in Fiskesjö's article, that it's not your ordinary criminal that is usually put on TV in such a spectacle (although that happens too from time to time), but those that may influence opinion contrary to the wish of the party – intellectuals, journalists, celebrities, lawyers, rights defenders and others.

As China has developed a system of laws for ruling the country, few have paid attention to the fact that it seeks not to create any rule of law, but rather a tool for stability to ensure economic growth on the one hand, and a tool for social control on the other. It may be naïve to think there was ever any real commitment to creating a system of Rule of law, but by bringing back the use of televised confessions in this more modern form, any such illusion should finally be shattered.

Hand in Hand: Chinese media and the police

Some journalists collaborating with police in this manner will likely claim innocence. They may claim ignorance at what precedes these recordings, that they simply don't know what treatment goes on before the victim agrees to do it. But they can't possible think that it's voluntary. One such journalist is Dong Qian, who has conducted several of these "interviews" for CCTV. An appeal by one her victim's – activist WuGan - has gone unanswered.

These are arguments that have always been flawed, and if as a journalist you claim to not know what goes on inside RSDL or pre-trial detention, or how people can just come out and denounce themselves or loved ones, the ignorance needed for such a statement is such that you are more or less disqualified to be taken seriously. The fact that anything read out will be prepared, sometimes with large cue cards or even LED screens, fully visible to the journalist, would make the true nature abundantly clear. And in some cases, the journalist themselves will be given prepared questions on a piece of paper to read from. On top of that, Chinese judicial authorities themselves have acknowledged on multiple occasions that torture and false confessions are widespread. After the release of *Scripted and Staged*, any argument of ignorance or simply not knowing moved from being flawed to outright ridiculous [the report was also released in a Chinese language edition].

The role of the media that collaborates with Chinese police, until recently limited to mainland Chinese state media, will be explored in Chapter 10. With Gui Minhai's third confession, the first non-Chinese language media, the *South China Morning Post* (SCMP), joined the ranks of media collaborating with the Chinese police. Editor in Chief Tammy Tam has failed to disavow the practice, or take any responsibility, even when faced with questions by Gui's daughter. Later on, CEO Gary Liu doubled down on their defense, claiming they had to partake to get a photo of Gui next to the guards. Both have failed to answer whether they were aware, or at least suspicious, of the situation in which the victim did the confession, or the treatment that likely preceded it. It's also telling that SCMP also remains one of the very few major media covering China that has not covered the report

Scripted and Staged, nor the phenomenon of Forced TV Confessions as such.

The closing chapter furthermore takes a look at the massive re-organization of Chinese media outlined in 2018 and the billions poured into overseas expansion, the crown-jewel to be the 350 journalist-strong production center soon to open in London, to provide the UK and EU-tailored broadcasting in scope that will make Russian state-TVs attempt at disinformation, propaganda and sewing division look like a shoe-string operation.

The chapter analyses Chinese media's re-organization side by side with the changing scope of the United Front Work Department (UFWD), and the role Chinese media plays in China's stated strategy of expanding its influence abroad. It also looks at another trend, namely that of how the CCP has moved to silence independent Chinese language media outside its borders, in Australia, North America, and Europe. Finally, alternative strategies, used primarily in Africa, with investment and purchase of local media, is put in the context of the greater global campaign to increase the CCPs influence.

Finally, it looks at the challenges posed to foreign media in both covering the use of Forced TV Confessions, but also the challenge that expanded operations of China's state/party– owned and controlled media poses in the new countries it establishes itself in. In an environment of few job openings and diminished pay – CCTV and other Chinese media steps in – offering steady and above average pay for journalists, the only caveat being that those journalists will have to learn how to forget their training, and instead take on a new role – PR workers for the Chinese Communist Party.

--

PETER DAHLIN (彼得达林) | Peter was one of the co-founders of 'China Action' in 2009, a small Chinese NGO that worked, until its forced closure in 2016, to develop a support infrastructure for Chinese rights defense lawyers, provide training for local 'barefoot' lawyers, and which numerous legal aid stations across China providing pro-bono legal assistance to victims of unlawful government actions. Following Peter's detention and placement into 'Residential Surveillance at Designated Location' (RSDL), and later his deportation on the grounds of the Espionage Law, he co-founded Safeguard Defenders, a pan-Asian human rights NGO supporting small civil society actors and which promotes and protects the Rule of law. Peter now lives in Spain, after spending over a decade in China and Southeast Asia.

TRIAL BY MEDIA
China's new show trials, and the global expansion of Chinese media

Chapter 2

Rights Defender ZHAI YANMIN

PROLOGUE

Zhai Yanmin (翟岩民) is a rights defender who still lives in China, and one of the first people detained in what became the "709 crackdown". Zhai himself is not a lawyer, unlike most other victims of the "709 crackdown", but an activist supporting both those lawyers, and the larger rights defense community, in general.

After being detained and tortured, he only gave in and agreed to make a televised confession after police threatened that they would capture his son. That threat was used continuously throughout his time in RSDL and later during imprisonment to force him to cooperate and make more televised confessions. The experience of making the confessions, in which he was forced to discredit friends, has wounded him psychologically, to the point of considering suicide.

Like many, he participated in the Tiananmen Square protests of 1989. Seeing many of his friends being taken by police due to their involvement in those protests, Zhai decided to strive for a low profile, focusing on raising his son. Over the past two decades, Zhai has worked in the tourism industry, as a taxi driver, and opened small businesses. Zhai stepped into human rights work shortly after the 2008 Olympics and the Charter 08 movement, which lead to Nobel peace prize winner Liu Xiaobo's imprisonment, and later, death.

Zhai Yanmin

About a week into the detention, the officer in charge of me, who was called Mr. Yang, told me that no one had been able to hold out for seven days before. Then he yelled out to someone outside: Go and get Zhai Yanmin's son! When I heard him say this I was stunned, they had found my weak spot. I'm very close to my son, you could say that we rely on each other for our very survival. My son is naïve and timid, and he'd never had any trouble with the police before.

I jumped up and told that Yang that this matter had nothing to do with my son. He said: "We decide whether it has something to do with your kid or not!" Then he went on: "Old Zhai, I'm going to give you 10 minutes to think about it: will you cooperate with us or will you make your son come here and join you!" He left as soon as he'd finished speaking. It's hard to put into words how conflicted I felt – my son had already had a hard life being born into this family, I just couldn't let anything happen to make him suffer further. Yet, I knew they wanted me to "confess", to hurt others, to use me. In the end, the choice was easy.

...they would use five or six electric batons to beat me.

About 10 minutes later, Yang came back, bringing with him a group of people. He said: "Old Zhai, have you thought it over yet?" I replied that as long as they didn't touch my son, I'd cooperate with them. I'd cooperate, but just don't make me incriminate or defame others. He said: "Old Zhai, you've made the right decision. If you'd decided to cooperate with us earlier, then you wouldn't have needed to suffer over the past seven days."

During my time inside, from RSDL to pre-trial detention, I was tortured in so many ways. They cuffed my hands behind my back, they locked me to iron railings, they would use five or six electric batons to beat me. For a long period they didn't let me eat, or drink water, or go to the bathroom. They subjected me to so many kinds of torture. Yet, it was nothing compared with their threats that they would detain my son.

Yang was holding some printed papers and he asked me to sign them. I asked to read them first. He said: "You have to sign them whether you read them or not, so what use is there in reading them?" I thought he was right, if I read it and then didn't sign it they'd grab my son. I didn't read them and signed them all. Later, anytime I didn't cooperate with them, they'd always start with the threats to my family.

Before all this, they hadn't let me sleep for several days and nights. Yang had tried to make me agree to make the video by telling me I wouldn't be allowed to sleep until I did. The guards at the detention center where I was kept at first were working with them. In the night-time when they'd come and get me for interrogation, they'd shine a strong light on my face, strong enough to burn my skin if it went on for too long. Then at four in the morning they'd take me back to my cell where I had another two hours of "duty", meaning I was not allowed to sleep. In those early days I had no more than 30 minutes sleep at any given time. That lack of sleep meant I had trouble remembering the exactly what they wanted me to say; that's why they eventually wrote it down for me to read from.

--

When making the televised confession I was in RSDL[1]. I was kept alone, in solitary confinement. It would go on for six months. In

---

[1] Zhai would go on to make three separate confessions, the first one while in detention (2016-06-22), the second (2015-07-12) and third (2015-07-19) ones while in RSDL.

comparison, my time prior to RSDL, in a detention center, felt like heaven – at least you shared a cell, could talk to people. Sitting alone in solitary confinement every minute could feel like an eternity.

Before we did the TV confession, police wrote down my answers, gave me the paper, and told me to read and memorize them. If during one of the many recordings I spoke my own truth, didn't follow the answers they had written for me, they'd immediately stop. Before it all got started officer Yang would come in every day to ask if I'd memorized it all yet and said if I couldn't, they'd think of another way.

While recording with CCTV I couldn't always remember my line, so they had a huge LED monitor put up in front of me.

After practicing a few days in my cell, we started to record. Every time before we recorded I would change into clothes that they'd prepared for me. They'd make me take medicine and they'd take off my handcuffs. They told me I needed the medicine for my heart problem, but when I got out and checked with a doctor, they said there was nothing wrong with my heart. Every time when they brought medicine, it never came with any sign, only pill themselves, so I never knew what the medicine really was. The so-called heart medicine they gave to me made me feel excited, I felt like talking. After taking the pills, once they started talking to me, I couldn't control my feeling of wanting to talk. But then again, at other times, the medicine made me sleepy instead. They gave me many kinds of pills to take every day, mostly to control my will or feeling. They would tell me that they checked that I have this and that problem, so the medicine is for my own good, I had to take it. Eat it! They would also double check if I took it for real.

Besides reading the words they had prepared for me, they told me I had to look sincere, at other times I had to look repentant.

I made six such recordings in total. Five of those times was with just police and their own camera crew, sometimes as many as a dozen people involved. The other time it was both police and media. When I saw her I knew that I knew her, that I'd seen her, her face. She introduced herself as Dong Qian, a journalist from CCTV. There were also some others there, from some newspapers, but I do not know who they were. Each journalist would take turns, asking me a question. They asked them freely [had no visible paper they read from], but the questions they asked all corresponded with the answers I had been forced to memorize. So I just had to connect their questions to the right answers. When we made the TV recording with the media it didn't take place at the same location, but instead I was black-hooded and taken downstairs and driven somewhere. I think it took about 20 minutes. I could only see again once sitting inside another room, only then did they take off my hood.

While recording with CCTV I couldn't always remember my line, so they had a huge LED monitor put up in front of me, but behind the camera, and the answer would appear there. On top of that, when I couldn't remember, the police would lean in and say that "all the other people" [detained in connection with the same case] were recording, and they were doing fine. If I didn't do well, I would be the one to get into trouble.

Before we got started with yet a new take police would remind me about my son, about what would happen if I didn't cooperate. The journalists who interviewed me didn't have much expression on their faces; I couldn't say that they were sympathetic or that they were heartless.

TRIAL BY MEDIA
China's new show trials, and the global expansion of Chinese media

The recording took place in a big rectangular meeting room, there were lots of people sitting on sofas all around.

Questions went from *how did I get to be on this path*, to *how did I get involved* and *much money did I earn from doing these kinds of things*. I remember it didn't take too long. My interrogators told me that the boss wasn't happy with that recording. When I got back to my cell I wasn't allowed to eat, or drink water, or go to the toilet - as a punishment. After some hours I had soiled myself. They were not happy because in that recording, unlike the other ones, they wanted me to name names. To denounce and incriminate others - the one thing I had told them before I wouldn't do. They told me I had to say that because they had arranged it all; "Do you want to do it, or do you want us to take your son?" they threatened me, but I refused.

They kept doing more recordings for about a week. I assume their superiors were not happy, or that it was clear I really didn't want to say what they told me to say. They said I just needed to remember the words, to not look directly at the camera, to try to look more natural. If it wasn't done right they'd start again and we repeated this again and again until we'd finished.

"You won't be able to stand it, just try. Since you agreed to cooperate, you must submit completely to us."

There were many cameras, not just one or two, and microphones, pointed at me. One time, the interrogation team was there and lots of high ranking security officers. They took turns to ask questions, my answers were those that I had memorized days before. Before going in, officer Hu kept threatening and intimidating me – he warned me that if I made any mistakes, they'd immediately go and detain my son.

Every time we recorded they took off my handcuffs and I changed into the clothes they had prepared – civilian clothing.

Sometimes if they weren't happy with the recording they'd take me out and talk to me for a bit, told me not to be nervous and just say what I'd memorized before. Sometimes I just couldn't remember, I think it was a side effect of the medicine, and often my mind would go blank not long after I returned to my cell.

They told me their job was to make my name stink so that no one would touch me afterward. They told me to cooperate with them and show my repentance. They said they would do whatever it takes. "You won't be able to stand it, just try. Since you agreed to cooperate, you must submit completely to us."

--

Later on - while I was no longer in RSDL but in a detention center awaiting trial - they kept telling me that I needed to mentally prepare myself for my sentencing - I was going away for a very long time. So, I prepared myself to go to jail for many years. They kept saying that I was a leader.

While in RSDL there was a period when they kept coming every day for "ideological study", where they tried to get me to understand how serious my "criminal actions" were. They said they had known about our every move for years. They wanted me to fully understand my role, and I had to confess, repent and cooperate with them, otherwise I would just sit in jail for the rest of my life, and my family would be implicated too.

I never heard who was the leader behind the scenes [who ordered the confessions], but I did hear that some top security officers were going to be watching my courtroom trial. They told me how I'd perform that day [at trial] would determine what would happen to me.

It was two weeks before my trial when one of my interrogators told me what was coming. They gave me a few pieces of paper, with answers written on it. Memorize it they told me. It was like the television recording all over again. Except, they told me, this is for your trial – there are no retakes. They told me to memorize every single word, and make sure to not hesitate, no pauses, speak smoothly, and make sure to memorize the questions the judge was going to ask me. Again, to connect my answers with his questions.

If I followed their instruction and performed well during the trial, I would definitely be dealt with leniently. In the last 10 days before my trial the prosecutor, Mr. Gong, would come to visit me in the detention center many times, just to check in on how well I was memorizing my answers, to check if I answered correctly, with correct impression and tone.

A week or so before the trial personnel from both the Procuratorate [prosecutor's office] and the court came to visit. Together we - prosecutor Mr. Gong, Judge Mr. Cai, and me, the defendant - had a test trial. Question and answers practiced. Everything that happened at the real trial – the questions asked, my answers given – were the same as during this test trial.

--

Later, after being released on bail [Zhai was given a three year suspended sentence], and got home I heard that they had harassed my son on several occasions - they said it was to help with my "ideological work" and they threatened him that they might detain him too.

If asked to give advice to others faced with similar a situation I think the choice depends on your family situation and your personality. If you think you can stand it, then persevere until the end.

Don't be like me, don't suffer only to later confess anyway.

Everything I said they had written down for me to say. Some of the things [they got me to say] were things I didn't know anything about, but I still had to follow the script; it was all according to their line of thinking. I had no choice.

I do want to add something - I didn't proactively sell anyone out. Not a single sentence was something of mine. I told them my bottom line was that I wouldn't sell anyone out. They said there were some things I had to say. I told them I didn't know anything about this, they said that they didn't care whether I knew about it or not, I had to read it out loud.

After my release, and thinking about what I went through, and imagining what others [connected to the "709 crackdown" who also made TV confessions] went through, I think all of us should have more contact and more communication, especially those of us who have made CCTV confessions, so that we can understand each other and support each other more, and stand up again.

We spent such a long time and recorded so much, but in the end they only broadcast a tiny portion. Although I never dare to watch the whole video in full, I have seen some clips, and surprisingly it seems they never aired anything from the video we made with CCTV and the other media – only the ones made with police. But for sure they edited and cut it. My small part was edited together and became part of a bigger story. I didn't watch the whole video because I feel such shame. I feel I can't face my former colleagues and my friends in the human rights community. There was a time I wanted to kill myself. I heard about people questioning me, blaming me, and criticizing me.

After my release I made a post on social media, apologizing, but the police found me almost right away, and told me to delete it. I did.

I knew the police would never let me explain publicly, and I remained quiet for such a long time.

Today when I look back, I think they made us go on TV to confess for three reasons:

One, to suppress us and others who they felt were somehow opposed to the government, and to show what can happen to people like us, to show the horrifying results of standing up.

Two, to take down the "leaders" of the greater community, to destroy these people's reputation, to make sure people do not trust them.

Three, to threaten the larger community, to make sure others would not dare to speak up against the government again.

I do my best trying not to explain it away or find excuses. Until now, I have spoken little about it, instead trying to undo the damage they did to me, but I know it will be difficult, perhaps more than difficult, but I have no choice but to try.

Zhai Yanmin

EPILOGUE

Zhai went on to describe his life after release:

"After I was released, I did some small work here and there, just trying to make a living, to feed myself and my family. I worked as taxi driver and did other small jobs. "

Zhai spoke about the inability to make even a basic living, feeling police would interfere to make sure whatever he did was sabotaged. And no longer being able to work to help others, to be a rights defender, he felt his identity slipping away. He even confided he had seriously thought about suicide, held back primarily because of his family.

"Then I got sick, and pretty bad too. Ever since the beginning of this year I have not been able to work at all, living off whatever friends can offer in help and support. Even though it has been a long time, I still get shaken and scared thinking back at my time in RSDL, and I live with both anxiety and memory loss today.
I tried to do some rights work when I first was released, but after I got sick I had to give it all up – my doctor tells me it would be a great risk if I ever get put through something like this again. "

TRIAL BY MEDIA
China's new show trials, and the global expansion of Chinese media

Chapter 3

Professor **LIU SIXIN**

PROLOGUE

Liu Sixin (刘四新) is a former teacher, researcher and doctor of law, now aged 52. He worked first as a lawyer before starting an academic career at the University of Zhejiang.

In 2009 he assaulted a university leader who had sexually abused Liu's wife. Liu also filed a lawsuit against the university leader. In the end, it was Liu who was imprisoned, for nearly five years, for "extortion" and intentional injury. What Dr. Liu considers a gross miscarriage of justice also pushed him towards rights defense work.

Dr. Liu had started working with more politically sensitive legal cases and had become involved in human rights law. Having lost his license because his criminal conviction, he was hired by Feng Rui Law Firm as a legal assistant. Due to his rights work, he was detained in 2014, but later released. He also published articles challenging state media's attempt to discredit the human rights lawyers' community, organized donation drives, and brought attention to key human rights cases.

Because of his connections to Feng Rui law firm and his work with human rights, he was one of the first lawyers detained when the 709 Crackdown began in the summer of 2015.

The raid

On the morning of July 10, 2015, I heard Zhou Shifeng had been taken [a lawyer with the same law firm as Liu]. Suddenly, more than a dozen police rushed into my home. Some were in uniform; others were in plainclothes. The leader, an older man, claimed he was from Tianjin police [a port city just east of Beijing where Liu lived and worked], and showed me a warrant for my detention. Strangely, it ordered me to be sent to Beijing No. 1 Detention Center. I say strange because it was the Tianjin city police who had broken into my home. I was accused of several crimes that were commonly used [for human rights cases] in recent years, that is picking quarrels and subverting state power. They asked me to sign my name on the warrant, but I refused. A young policeman in uniform said mockingly, "You're already in this situation, so why do you refuse to sign?" I continued to refuse. They handcuffed my hands behind my back, put a black hood over my head and ordered me to sit on the ground.

Knowing what had happened to [lawyers] Teng Biao, Li Heping, and Tang Jitian when they were taken during the "Jasmine Revolution" period in early 2011, it was clear I wasn't going to any detention center. They would put me in a black jail.

They roughly searched my place for about 20 minutes. They removed the hood, unlocked the cuffs and forced me to sign for a list of items they had confiscated from my place and had put into a small box. Then they quickly cuffed and hooded me again. Was strong-armed out, one person on my left, one on my right and I was put into a car. I was in the middle, with the two on either side of me. Some 40 minutes later we arrived at a detention center, probably the Beijing one, but after getting out of the car and waiting just a few minutes, I was put into another car and we drove for another 40 minutes. Once my hood was taken off, I saw that I was in a room. Based on the little I could hear, I think we were somewhere in the southeast of Beijing.

They took all my clothes and told me to show them my ass so they could inspect me. After they had finished, my clothes given back, they explained the rules. I had to sit in a chair placed in the middle of the room. There was a window, but a heavy curtain covered it. The walls, the window frame, everything, was padded [to prevent suicide]. It was obvious that this place was one of the legendary "shuanggui" facilities[2] [Liu had been placed in RSDL].

I would stay in this facility for two months, and then four more months in a similar one in Tianjin. For six months I never saw sunlight and did not talk to anyone except my interrogators.

Interrogation

There were two main interrogators, but the older one did most of the talking; the other one rarely opened his mouth. The main interrogator didn't tell me his name in the beginning. After a few months, after I was transferred to another facility in Tianjin, he said his family name was Wang. During the two months I was in Beijing, he questioned me mostly about the dinner meetings our group of lawyers held. He particularly wanted to know information about the people who came to them—they were the ones that had also been taken by the police [many of these people represented the core of the 709 crackdown targets].

---

[2] A former system for detaining communist party members accused of discipline breaches or corruption, outside the legal system, always incommunicado and in solitary confinement. Similar to RSDL, which is largely based on the system, but for anyone, not just party members. Shuanggui has now been replaced by Liuzhi.

Four or five days in, in the nighttime, they tried to get me to tell them the password to my cellphone. I didn't have anything in the phone that was that important but there were some photos I had taken with friends, which I didn't want them to see. Interrogator Wang got angry. At around eleven that night, he started walking up to me, aggressively, as if he was about to hit me. When he got right up to me, instead of a beating, he just bumped his fist against my chest. A younger officer was standing close by, pointing to my chest. "You know, even if you don't tell us, we'll find a way to get into your phone." This went on for a while, until I gave up and gave them my password.

Later on, [when Wang wanted something from me,] he would say: "If you don't cooperate, we'll bring a rack [bench] here. With a single order, I could get someone to take off all your clothes and make you stand on the rack naked for several days." "If you think the chair is too comfortable, I will change it to an iron chair." I replied, "Do you mean tiger chair? I sat on one of those before, last time I was in jail."

Wang hinted that they had a mole in the human rights lawyers' community, to feed them all the information they needed, so that they could strike at everyone in one go. "Don't you know that we can make you disappear?" Every once in a while, pretty often actually, Wang would say that in the past the international community, the United States, would try to help, to defend me and people like me. But not anymore, not now China is powerful. "Do you think people are intervening on your behalf now? No. China doesn't need to care anymore. We've taken more than 300 of you now. So how this ends is entirely up to you."

On August 27, there was some changes in the interrogation team. Another policeman, also from Tianjin, took over. He would be my interrogator from now until I was released on bail over a year later. "We can do everything and anything to you here [RSDL]. My boss told me to use some 'measures' on you. I told him Liu Sixin doesn't need it, not yet." I asked, "Do you mean to torture me?" My directness left him speechless.

At eight at in the evening, on September 8, I was transferred to Tianjin. Things were about to become a lot worse.

For the first few days, I would be sat in a normal chair, but one morning I noticed it had been moved and replaced with a new seat. I had suffered on one of these before and so I knew what was coming. It was a round stool with a very small and thin top. After I got up from bed the guard in the room said: "You're not allowed to sit on the chair anymore, from now on use the stool." I had to sit on that stool all day. The interrogator did not show up. The stool was very high so that only my toes just scraped the floor [so all the weight was on Liu's back and legs]. It didn't take long for the pain to start, with my feet dangling in the air and all my body weight on that small seat. An old wound in my waist was the first part of my body to start feeling the agony. I wondered if they were using the same 'measure' on Wang Yu, Li Shuyun, and Wang Fang too [female rights lawyers]? Or Hu Shigen or Zhou Shifeng, who were older than me, and who already have health problems.

"You should say what I tell you to say; you'll get your chance only if you do this."

My interrogator appeared the second day. As he walked in, he teased me: "How was the stool? Was it comfortable?" After I told him the pain I was in he said: "I'll talk to the leader of the guards. I'll tell him not to make you sit on it again." He was trying to look kind and helpful.

They would use other 'measures' on me. They starved me by serving me smaller portions of food at mealtimes. After the "dangling stool", they started the food deprivation. The first time this happened, the police officer turned his head to the guard and said: "If he doesn't cooperate, we can cut his rations even more or even stop them altogether."

Sometimes, the guard would not let me eat the food that was served. I had to stare at it, while it went cold. Sometimes they didn't give me any water. Another punishment was to prevent me from showering, especially in the late summer when I was in Beijing and it was very hot.

CCTV

During a period of about a year I was "interviewed" and recorded six times. During the first six months I was not even formally arrested.

On the morning of July 13, just three days after I had been detained [while kept in Beijing], Wang said: "Let's skip the chat. It's been arranged for you and others to record a video. This is your chance. We're not giving this change to Hu [Shigen] or Zhou [Shifeng] even if they want it. We weren't going to let [lawyer] Li Heping either, but we will now. [No TV confession from Li Heping was ever broadcast, but Zhou was made to do one]. You need to draw a line between yourself and Hu, and the problems with Zhou." I told him I'd only met Hu a few times over dinner and I didn't know him.

"You should say what I tell you to say; you'll get your chance only if you do this." I told him I didn't know much about Zhou's personal life, only that he likes to drink. Wang said they already knew about his personal life. "He leads a very immoral personal life, doesn't he?" As he was leaving, I asked him if the recording would be broadcast on TV. He answered vaguely. "The boss didn't mention anything about putting it on TV. This is just for our internal documentation, it won't be put on TV."

Hours later Wang came back. "Li Heping has finished his recording' he did very well. The boss is very satisfied. You should take this chance as well."

I was black hooded, and like before, two people led me to a car. A short drive later we entered a building. By the time my black hood was removed we were in a room. I was made to sit in a tiger chair and they locked the board over my legs.

We started recording but after the first take Wang was not happy. "You spoke haltingly with no feeling. I taught you how to say it, didn't I?" Wang said. We started over. "I will never again be involved in any right defense events. I will not publish any information online, and I will not be in touch with petitioners anymore." I said. I had to distance myself from Hu and talk about how Zhou likes to drink and that he spends lots of money on expensive things.

Wang looked at a superior who was present: "Shall we record one more?" "No, this is fine," he responded.

That evening, back at the cell, Wang came back. "Our boss watched the video. He's not satisfied. Too bad you didn't do it well, you lost your chance."

As my hood was removed I saw her. It was Dong Qian from CCTV.

Two days later, he came back. "We decided to give you one more chance. This time CCTV will make it. They specialize in making these for the police's internal procedures." I immediately thought of Gao Yu [a well-known journalist who had been forced to make a TV confession in 2014]. I responded right away, "I won't go on TV." "They're not real journalists, they just make internal productions for the leaders of the central government," Wang said.

The same thing happened but this time I was put in a different room, probably in another building, because the drive was much longer. I heard Wang say: "Liu Sixin is here, I don't know if he recognizes you". As my hood was removed I saw her. It was Dong Qian from CCTV. She looked smaller than on TV. There were more than a dozen people in the room and a professional TV camera. I sat down. Dong Qian sat in front of me. She was making an effort to look serious, like a judge.

"What kind of person is Zhou Shifeng?" "Does Zhou behave as a professional lawyer?" "How do his legal skills compare with yours?" "He has lots of experience" I said. When prodded further, I admitted I wasn't very impressed with his legal skills. Over a year later, when I first saw the video they had used on TV, I saw that they had cut this one line out of the whole thing and used in a TV news piece attacking Zhou.

"Why does he hate the government so much?" Dong Qian asked.

I tried to respond: "[the] lawyers are just unhappy about corruption, it's not about hating the government." "Not really, what Zhou Shifeng said at Qiweishao restaurant [the restaurant for the dinner gatherings], didn't sound like someone only unhappy about the corruption." she retorted.

They wanted me to say things that could be used against Zhou. [Zhou was the head of the law firm Feng Rui, where many of the key rights defense lawyers, including Liu, worked]

Another woman took over after a while. After some more questions, Dong Qian told her and the others in the room: "Wang Yu's arrived, let's finish up here. We can do it again if necessary."

Two days later, I did it again. Same process, same room, but different journalists. There were four or five of them. Again, they wanted material on Zhou. This time it was a male journalist. I met him again a year later when he came to interview me. This time, he said: "Zhou Shifeng hired so many stubborn lawyers for his law firm. What was he after?" "Other law firms didn't hire lawyers like Wang Yu and Wang Quanzhang, why did Zhou?" I told him any lawyer needed approval from the judicial bureau to practice.

"Most law firms don't take cases related to demolitions or Falun Gong, why do these lawyers take these kinds of cases?" They didn't approve of my answers. "He didn't have any other purpose, at most, it was to get famous." I had said. Wang interjected: "Stop beating around the bush. Just say straight out what Zhou wanted to do."

I said: "I haven't been at Feng Rui Law Firm that long. At most I thought he wanted to build up a reputation."

A female journalist said: "The interrogator told me about your situation. That you're convinced that your case [the reason why Liu has been put in prison] was unjustly handled. We'll report your situation to the upper levels, but we can't promise anything. What you need to do now is to cooperate with your interrogator." Obviously, these journalists were doing the police's job.

--

After this it was almost another year before they started "interviewing" me again. By that point I had been formally arrested and had finished my six months in RSDL. I was being held in Tianjin No. 2 Detention Center.

I was black hooded again and taken outside. But this time [we must have just moved to a new building] we just walked down some hallways before arriving in a room. It looked like a standard single hotel bedroom. This must be where more senior people are kept when detained. Wang wasn't there, but the junior interrogator was, along with two others. "They're from the police news center. They're here to record a video of you." Just like before I said I would not do it if it was for TV. "They're from a police department. If it was for TV, it wouldn't be us filming it," the junior interrogator said. "I promise, this won't be put on TV" one of the other police officers said.

They took out a script three pages long and told me to memorize it. Most of it was based on my previous interrogations. I remember reading one line: "Zhou Shifeng is just an old fox." Other parts seemed to have no specific target and were vague. I made some notes and pointed out small things that I didn't want to say or that should be changed. "Our boss has decided on the script," the junior interrogator said, but when I got it back before the recording, some of my changes had been made.

The interrogator told the other officers: "He used to be a university professor, he's given lectures so it won't be difficult for him to record this." They put the script on my knees and started recording. After a "failed" first take, they seemed satisfied with the second.

Mostly I had to speak about my advocacy work, and use of social media to spread information. They also wanted me to talk about why Zhou had hired Wang Yu and Wang Quanzhang and why he had worked with Wu Gan [an activist also detained and later imprisoned in the same crackdown]. I said that Zhou hired them to boost his reputation in the community. I added some details, which were not in the script, about my own case [in 2009]. They did not want this in the video so we had to rerecord. We filmed the whole thing, exactly the same, but I wasn't allowed to mention my case. I was helpless.

--

Not long after I made my final recording. It was sixth. This time, we left the detention center. When my handcuffs were removed and the black hood was taken off, I saw the same male journalist from a year ago. "'I saw you last year" I said. He made an awkward expression. Four others were present; they looked like senior leaders. I figured they were in charge of all the investigations into the [709] lawyers.

The male journalist said: "I'm asking you one more time, why did Zhou Shifeng hire people like Wu Gan. What did he want?" I replied angrily: "You all know that my previous case was unjust but none of you have done anything about it." They ignored me. He continued: "What did you do at the Feng Rui Law Firm?" I felt this question was the key one and would decide my fate – whether or not I went to prison. I told them "I didn't have a lawyer's license anymore. I couldn't do court work. I could only write documents." One of the four men interrupted me. "It looks like you still don't understand that you made a mistake. You're still not admitting your guilt". Another said: "We came here because you've confessed before.". And a third: "We heard your English is good. Did you translate documents?"

"You lawyers only believe in the law. You don't know anything about politics," my interrogator said. "Let's ask him." One of the senior men who hadn't spoken before said: "Forget it, we're done here."

On the way back my interrogator asked me, "Are you going to confess or not? Do you want to get out of here?"

Since I'd been taken, my interrogators had told me over and over again that their boss had said that "all those who met at the Qiweishao Restaurant [the common venue for lawyers' dinners] need be dealt with. And Hu and Zhou need be dealt with severely." Now he was saying that it was possible that some of us could be dealt with more leniently. And that the recordings would be used to decide on how to deal with all of the lawyers who had been taken.

Confession

For the first two months Wang never asked me to confess. It wasn't until I was transferred to Tianjin that another interrogator suddenly said: "Do you confess?" I knew they would ask me this eventually. I stayed silent. He continued, "You must understand your case will be decided on whether you confess or not. Don't just think about the law or talk about the law. This is not something that can be solved by the law." Earlier, he had said: "The things you did with those lawyers and with the petitioners, well the boss says, they will never be allowed again. We have to crack down on this and punish everyone severely."

They took out a script three pages long and told me to memorize it.

It reminded me of how things were done during the Cultural Revolution. They said: "What's important is for the boss to see your good attitude when you confess." I steeled my heart and said: "I confess." He wrote my confession down on a piece of paper. "You already know this is not a legal issue."

The same night I lay in bed unable to sleep. I believed that my confession would mean more lenient treatment, but the shame of confessing was extremely painful. Before I was detained, I had been planning my parents' 70th birthday party and preparing the final papers for appealing my earlier conviction. The last time I was sent to prison my son was about to finish middle school. His final exams didn't go as well as they should have, and he lost enough points to deny him a place at the high school he wanted. I was sure this was because his father was in prison. When I was released, he was already a freshman at university. I just wanted to be released as soon as possible. Despite this, I would struggle with confessing.

By August, more than a year since I had been snatched from my home, they had exhausted their investigation. One day they told me to "write a letter, showing your understanding of things. It must be detailed. It's very important, and will be shown to the boss. Based on this, we will decide your case." I racked my brains and wrote for two days. Why did they charge me with "picking quarrels", and "subverting state power"? When they saw my letter they told me to delete a part about corruption. "The boss will not like it," they said. "You should write about how, if we give you a chance, you promise never to contact the stubborn lawyers, petitioners, or the media." "The title of your writing should be 'repentance letter'."

The final stretch

By November the first year, having spent almost half a year in solitary confinement, I gave up on the fantasy that I would get out anytime soon. I had no idea what was going to happen next, what they might do.

By December, I had decided I would refuse to confess at my trial. If I refused, they'd only have the interrogation notes to use against me. It was early the next month, January 2016, when I was officially arrested. I was transferred to a pre-trial detention center. I went through a complicated security procedure before being placed into cell C110. I was made to wear a scarlet prison uniform, for "our kind of prisoners." It was different from the other vests worn by most others. It meant I was under stricter monitoring. I was no longer in solitary confinement, like the first six months, but because I had the scarlet vest, the other cellmates had been told not to talk to me. The same policeman who had delivered my meals when I was in RSDL, the one who had starved me, and threatened to cut off all me food, was also handing out food at the detention center. Later on I learned his name was Yuan Yi, but only after some other cellmates had bravely started to talk with me.

Not long after being transferred to the detention center, my interrogator told me my case had been decided and I would be assigned a lawyer. I knew they would never allow me to appoint my own lawyer, but I requested it anyway. "You're not allowed. We will appoint one for you. Some of the others have met with their assigned lawyers and it has worked out well," he said. I met with the two lawyers assigned to me in the end. One had his own law firm in Tianjin. Once I started meeting these lawyers, my interrogations started up again.

In March [2016] they started asking me about every little detail about my life right back to when I was in elementary school. They had been ordered to "investigate my history." Around the same time, I was allowed outside to take some exercise for the first time in my detention and I saw sunlight – the first time in over eight months. I became more convinced I should not confess at my trial. I started paying attention to news reports about us lawyers. They used to broadcast CCTV news in the cell. In January, I had seen Wang Qiushi [a lawyer] confess. It was obvious he had just memorized some script. Some of the things he said, some of the expressions, were old-fashioned, such as how he said anti-China forces from the West had used him. I also saw Peter Dahlin [Chapter 5]. The presenter claimed he had confessed to everything. The cell leader looked at me strangely after that news program with Peter's confession. Shortly afterwards, the cell leader was called outside, when he came back he said all those prisoners wearing scarlet vests – that is us lawyers -- were no longer allowed to watch the TV news. It also meant the others in the cell couldn't watch the news anymore either.

--

July 29 the interrogator told me: "The boss has decided to let you testify." Shortly afterwards, I was taken to another room in the detention center. My main interrogator, and seven or eight uniformed police officers were sat waiting for me. I sat down. Opposite me sat the prosecutor, a man called Gong Ning. A policeman took out a paper with my testimony written down for me. Gong said: "Dr. Liu, take a look and get ready to testify in court."

I read the few paragraph. Nothing on there was what I said during my interrogations. The words were all attacking Zhou. They wanted me to say that Zhou had blackened the legal system.

I said: "I can't testify like this. Speaking these meaningless words is not testifying. Please list the specific things he did which blackened the judicial system." An older policeman said: "It's already been decided. You have to say exactly this."

"Then, I won't testify," I said.

He lost his temper and said: "You've read too many books!" Gong Ning said: "Dr. Liu, we've all read your articles and they are very learned. We all sympathize with you. But if you don't cooperate, we will have to reconsider how we handle your case."

Of course I wanted to go free but this "testimony" crossed a red line for me. I sat in silence for a while.

Gong Ning said: "You should reconsider. This is your chance. Even Wu Gan said Zhou Shifeng blackened the judicial system."

"So let Wu Gan testify in court," I said.

My main interrogator started to look worried. "Why have you changed your mind?"

"These words are meaningless. This is not testimony," I said.

"Forget it. He's not cooperating. Let's go," the older man said.

My main interrogator said he would try to talk me around, but the older one told him to forget about it

When I returned to my cell, I told myself that even if it meant I had to stay inside I would never testify in court like that.

--

On August 2 I was in the cell when the cell leader told someone to switch over to CCTV13 [state TV news channel] even though we were not allowed to watch the news. The guards outside were not paying much attention to us. The news reported that Zhai Yanmin [Chapter 3] had been given a three year suspended sentence. One of the other prisoners in my cell who had been transferred from the same detention center as Zhai said: "That's Zhai Tiancheng!" Zhai had been given the name Tiancheng when he was locked up, to conceal his real identity. I'd been given a fake name too – Liu Shunli. We were given false names so no one could find us. Technically, there was no one called Liu Sixin in my cell. I was not allowed to disclose my real name even to my cellmates.

TRIAL BY MEDIA
China's new show trials, and the global expansion of Chinese media

After this the police came back and yelled at me for not agreeing to testify. Later the same day I saw another news program that covered Hu Shigen's sentencing. A day later, I watched Zhou Shifeng's trial. And after that, Gou Hongguo [another related case].

The same day Gou's case was on the TV, the cell leader told me to pack my things. Not that I had anything to pack. I wondered why they were releasing me on bail. I told my cell mates my real name, just in case I would not get a chance to say goodbye. The next day, in the morning, a police officer yelled out: "Liu Shunli, come out!" As I left I met the director of the detention center.

"We've decided to release you even though you didn't cooperate because of the circumstances of your previous case." With that, I was released on bail. It had been a year, much of it in solitary confinement.

EPILOGUE

Dr. Liu was released on bail from Tianjin 2nd detention center on August 6, 2016, and like other 709 lawyers, he is still under monitoring, despite his bail conditions having been lifted a year after his release.

Following his release from his earlier imprisonment in 2013, when Liu started his path to rights defense work, he and his wife got a divorce, sold their home. The son now lives with his mother, to protect him from harassment and disturbance from the police.

Following his release on bail, Dr. Liu left Tianjin for Beijing. Having been placed under close watch, Liu now lives in a house in a village, the house having been arranged by the police themselves. The police have officers living nearby, having him under direct watch, and he is also arranged to eat with the same police.

Dr. Liu has tried to resume his academic career, by going abroad, to the United Kingdom, to continue his research and scholarship, but like many others, the Chinese state will not let him leave the country. He is forbidden from meeting or talking with other rights defenders, have contact with any outside organizations, nor speak with media. He is isolated, without work, with no immediate prospects, and is dependent on the police.

Liu Sixin

Chapter 4

Activist **LIU XING**

PROLOGUE

Liu Xing (刘星), from Hebei, a province that surrounds Beijing, who also goes by the name Laodao (老道), was one of the first victims of what was to become the "709 Crackdown". Liu was detained on June 15, 2015, and held at two different detention centers in Shandong province, and eventually sentenced to two years of imprisonment, released in the late spring of 2017.

Liu, with his distinctive long hair and thick glasses, helped organize petitioners to protest outside courthouses during trials of rights defenders.

Liu Xing grew up as an orphan, having lost his parents during an earthquake when he was a mere three years old. Since then, he has never had a "Hukou", a must-have registration that allows access to education, healthcare, and government services. He was raised by a Taoist priest until the priest died when Liu was 15, after which he started wandering, making a living for himself as a migrant worker. His first contact with rights defense work came when he was refused payment for some construction work he had done. Instead, the boss hired people to beat him up for complaining. He started meeting other rights defenders, going to bookstores for lectures from experts, and slowly become part of the rights defense community. He was leading a protest in Shandong province when he was detained.

Liu Xing

TRIAL BY MEDIA
China's new show trials, and the global expansion of Chinese media

I was taken to the detention center at around seven in the evening. When I look back now, it's obvious the raid had been planned in advance. There were dozens of police stationed outside the courthouse where we were protesting. There was no warrant, of course, I and some other rights defenders were thrown into police cars and driven off. I had been taken by the police when protesting unfair trials before and didn't think this would be any more serious than the many times before when they had detained me. Things turned out very differently, and I could never have imagined what was to come.

--

Once detained, I was taken to a cell in the Weifang [city] detention center [along the coast of Shandong province].

The special investigation team began interrogating me right away, using the shameless "exhausting the eagle" method. Namely: they took me to the interrogation room, locked me in [onto a tiger chair], ignored me, and didn't talk to me. They just stared at me and forced me to sit strapped onto the chair. When I wasn't in the tiger chair I was in a cell in the detention center I shared with some dozen others, but I was expressly forbidden from communicating or talking with anyone.

Sitting in the chair, as soon as I shut my eyes, they'd take a long rolled up piece of paper to poke me or tap me around the face. They wouldn't do anything really -- they just wouldn't let me sleep. That was how one night passed, it was only the next day at around six in the morning, when it was time for the prisoners in the cell to get up, that they sent me to the cell to eat breakfast. After eating, another guard took me back to the interrogation room. I was locked into the chair, again, and they carried on not speaking to me. Just, if they saw me close my eyes, they would shake and slap me. It carried on like this, day after day.

Around about 10 days later, I felt like I couldn't cope any longer. I felt dizzy the whole day. I couldn't control my limbs. I was just responding subconsciously to everything, but my heart was constantly reminding me that I must hold on! I suffered unspeakably. I just wanted to die. For this reason, I forced myself to go on a hunger strike to demand a break so I could rest. But, in response, they force-fed me through tubes, making my stomach bleed [gastrointestinal hemorrhage].

After they started speaking to me, actually interrogate me, lots of police officers came. They tried to coerce me to speak by offering to release others as a bargaining chip. They told me: "your case was ordered from high up, if you don't speak, there's no way you'll be allowed to leave, and others will also have to be detained. If you confess, we'll consider releasing the others." And then they said again: "It's already been more than 10 days now, even if you don't speak, others have already spoken. If you speak, it's only to confirm what statements others have made, and we will consider setting them free. You definitely won't be allowed to go free."

My body wasn't functioning; I was in a daze; my eyes were glassy. I was on the verge of collapse.

By this time, it was already July 1 - I remembered it clearly because it was Memorial Day for *the gang* [the anniversary of the founding of the Chinese Communist Party]. I had already been interrogated to exhaustion for 14 days. During those 14 days, I had only slept for a maximum of 30 minutes in any one go [continuously]. My body wasn't functioning; I was in a daze; my eyes were glassy. I was on the verge of collapse.

Given that the thugs claimed they would detain other people as a way to coerce me, and even more so because I clearly understood this gangster-ish political regime, I was sure that they would make good on all their threats: They really would do the most despicable and contemptible, the most vicious and shameless, acts. In the end I chose to break my silence.

All the above happened when I was in Shandong province's Weifang Detention Center. I was detained there from June 15, 2015, until December 14, 2016. I was accused of gathering a crowd to disrupt public order. Once the Procuratorate [prosecutor] took over my case, my crime changed to picking quarrels and provoking troubles, a similar but different charge.

I was transferred to another detention center in the same province, and later, after having been tried and sentenced, I was moved (January 14, 2017) to Shandong province's Tai'an Prison. I would stay in that prison until I was released later that year, on May 25.

During my time in prison I would be given medicine, according to them for blood pressure. It seemed important to them because they would stand next to me, to monitor that I really took the pills. From those I talked to, it seemed many others were being force-fed medication in a similar manner. Once released – and no longer being given the medicine, I started having severe memory loss, and my ability to focus almost disappeared. These symptoms remained with me for a year before getting better.

On the my 29th day of detention, after staying up all night for so many days in a row, and after being pressured to speak by being told that if I didn't then others wouldn't be allowed to go free, they brought it up – they told me I needed to make a video recording. It was never told it was for TV or public, just a video. It was for their boss, the higher up. The boss needed to be satisfied, and if so, the investigation would be over. I started thinking of how many of the people that had been taken had been so because of me, because I had organized the protests. I agreed.

Before this happened they had made me write letters, statements, showing that I repent. I had to, they would say, or other people would suffer the consequences. At first I had refused, since I had no crime to admit to, but later I did write it, taking two or three days to write and edit and rewrite. When time came for my TV recording, this was the material that was used.

...and said in front of the room full of journalists, that this was a video to be made and shown to their superiors.

When we went to record the video, I was told to take off the detention center clothing and change into the plainclothes my interrogators had bought (a summer t-shirt). After that, we changed rooms. I was taken to an office inside the detention center. It was a simple office, with only a table and chairs. There were a lot of people in the room who had journalist IDs, and many microphones were pointed in my direction. There were also professional cameras. I asked what was all this about? One of my interrogators answered, and said in front of the room full of journalists, that this was a video to be made and shown to their superiors. They kept up the lie to me, even in front of the journalists.

All in all, there were maybe seven or eight people in the room, two or three of them police, the rest from the media. This happened three times, and the composition of people would change somewhat. Each session would only take maybe 40 minutes, and the police and the journalists would all take turns asking questions, but the police were more active. Just like with the repentance letter, they wanted me to say into the camera that I had colluded with lawyers, had cheated with donations, that I had blackmailed local governments. These were not facts, and I told them that anyone, even as a criminal suspect, had basic rights. And in my case, all my work was merely to support others, to give them help, but they, of course, tried to twist my words. If someone I supported was corrupt, why should he get support! I told them even a murderer has rights. In the end, they let me answer my own way, and I admitted that I could have done thing better. If something [I said] was too far from what they wanted, they would stop, and order me to start again and say it differently, to do a retake.

While I was making one of my recordings, other people taken and involved in the same case were also making recordings in other rooms nearby. The interrogators went back and forth into the different rooms to check and ask about the progress, and if it was going according to plan.

--

It wasn't until I was released from prison much later – after having been prosecuted, tried, sentenced and then served my time – that I found out that my recording had been broadcast on TV, including on CCTV. Of course, the broadcast material had been heavily edited, with only the special negative parts kept. I definitely did not confess to a crime [on camera then], I just accepted some of the facts. The only real confession happened when I went on trial later.

Later on, a friend told me that the videos I and others had made, besides being broadcast on TV, was also being shown at petition offices. They were using the videos to scare petitioners, to say "look! This is what will happen to you if you cause trouble". Since I had worked with petitioners, and been one myself, I would hear about it. Some, disillusioned with the government might not believe it, and some that I knew wouldn't be so easily scared, but others are prone to believe what the government says, so when they said I had done what I did for money, when they defamed me, many certainly believed it.

I think the most frightening thing I can imagine is not the torture, but when they attack family members. For me, an orphan who never had any children, there were no children to attack, but they did attack my girlfriend Zhang Wanhe, and also threatened to block her daughter's education and destroy her future. In the end, me simply yielding to those threats would not have helped, and I did what I could to stay focused, to realize I had to stay truthful.

--

After I was released, I heard different people talking about me in the rights community. Some people thought it was a shame that I went on TV, others would badmouth me. More than that, I could feel how some people would distance themselves from me. I realize this response might be normal, but I wish they instead do the opposite, to ask, to talk, to communicate, so to learn how this happened, and why it happened. These TV confessions are made, and forced upon people to make, for a reason – to defame the person, to destroy them - and it seems to be something not everyone understands.

Each person has different ability to handle the effect [of these TV confessions], some can stand up again, some not. For a human rights defender, the most important thing really is that he or she knows what they want, that they continue to do in accordance with what they believe. For me, I don't really mind if they look down on me.

I know foreigners, and *the west*, can't really help China directly, but they can help. Why, with this practice, and many other things they do, do they continue to cooperate with such a regime, to help them continue these things? What good can come for them in the end by cooperating with this kind of regime?

Liu Xing

TRIAL BY MEDIA
China's new show trials, and the global expansion of Chinese media

EPILOGUE

Liu has made it clear that he does not have the intention to give up, to stop his work, to let them succeed.

> *Since my release, I remain committed to my work, to work for the public interest. It's not been easy – I do not have a Hukou [household registration] – and I cannot get one, so I cannot get an ID card – which means I have not been able to get any construction jobs. For now, I've been living off savings from my earlier jobs. Police told me that my hometown doesn't want to help me get a Hukou since I'm a "trouble-maker".*

The police's persecution of Liu, and others around him, have not stopped after his release. Liu says:

> *They continue to monitor me, setting up a surveillance camera outside my home. Most recently, they have done what they could to stop me marrying my girlfriend. A friend of mine, who himself was also forced to make a TV recording, was forcibly sent all the way to Inner Mongolia, just because he was supposed to be the host for our wedding, anything to stop our wedding party.*
> *As we decided to get married anyway police told us we had to leave, to "go travel". In the end, we both, along with our cat and dog, packed up and set out by car.*

Chapter 5

NGO Director **PETER DAHLIN**

PROLOGUE

Peter Dahlin (彼得 · 达林) is a Swedish human rights worker who moved to China in 2007 after some years working for the Swedish government. After some short-term volunteer work for a small NGO that folded when its leader, Hou Wenzhuo, had to go into exile, he and others, including lawyer Wang Quanzhang, started an NGO, 'China Action'.

Through 'China Action' Peter worked to provide critical support to China's besieged lawyer community, establishing an infrastructure for providing financial support to lawyers to work on politically sensitive cases, and launching support actions for lawyers persecuted for their work. It also organized a wide range of training programs for lawyers and 'barefoot' lawyers – China's frontline legal defenders who specialize in suing the government for wrongful actions, as well as establishing more than ten legal aid stations across China where 'barefoot' lawyers would provide legal support for public interest litigation.

In 2013 agents from the Ministry of State Security (MSS) spent six months trying to plant a mole in the organization. Starting in 2015, more and more partners were detained or placed in 'residential surveillance at a designated location' (RSDL). When almost two dozen MSS agents raided Peter's home in Beijing on the night of January 3, 2016, the raid was expected.

State Security Agent Zhang, who had taken to playing the "good cop" role while his colleague handled the "bad cop" act, arrived sometime after dinner time. "Have you had dinner yet?" he asked after entering my cell. He pulled up a chair next to my tiny bed; the two guards who would otherwise sit staring at me 24 hours a day, left. These cozy "fireside chats"—I called them this because they reminded me of [former US president] Franklin Roosevelt's World War II broadcasts, would happen every once in a while, and were a welcome break from the extreme boredom of solitary confinement, or the daily (or rather, nightly) intense five- to six-hour interrogations.

At this point, I'd spent some two or three weeks in a secret prison south of Beijing and had been accused of using foreign funding to subvert state power. The case was being handled by the Ministry of State Security. My girlfriend had been taken in the same raid, despite having no connection to my work, and was languishing in solitary confinement while they decided on my case. A long list of colleagues or partners were taken either in the same operation or had been taken one by one over the preceding six months. Almost everyone was disappeared—not arrested—and placed into solitary confinement under what they call Residential Surveillance at a Designated Location, a favorite new tool of suppression.

"I've just spent the whole day at court," Agent Zhang told me. "You know I have pushed very hard for them to find a diplomatic solution... I have pushed for this hard, as I think it's the best way to resolve the situation." He told me he was going back again tomorrow to see the panel of judges who were deliberating my case and were deciding whether to prosecute me or not. There was a chance they could arrange a diplomatic solution on medical grounds. I knew full well that this is not how the legal procedure is supposed to work in China, but then again laws are rarely worth the paper they are written on there, and I had no reason to doubt him.

This is how the lead up to the forced TV confession began.

--

The two to three weeks I'd spent inside this prison, which for technical reasons is not allowed to be called a prison, had taught me a lot already. I was probably better informed about what to expect than most, but I had often wondered how id react and behave should it ever happen. Making guesses in my head about how I would, or would not, act, if I would break, or not break, and all other related issues had all been mind games. At last, I was being put to an actual test. And as things progressed, there would be a number of those tests. The forced TV confession was but the last or final step.

"Things came to a head three or four days in, as I entered a showdown with Mr. Liu"

The first few days started well enough, and they took their time to map out my background, who I was, and just slowly prod a little bit about my work, the reason I was there. Things came to a head three or four days in, as I entered a showdown with Mr. Liu. If agent Zhang came to take the role of "good cop", Liu didn't only play the role of "bad cop" but seemed to have been born and breed for it. The round glasses, the ominous looking grin on his face, his relatively minor stature all reminded me of the Nazi leader in Raiders of the Lost Ark, a thought I have not been able to shake to this day.

Often they would intentionally misunderstand me, or change the wording of what I had said. I had to be on constant guard for such tiny details, easier said than done with little to no sleep and nightly non-stop interrogations. Liu had agreed that if I wrote down a basic overview of the work of my NGO, 'China Action', they would in return arrange a meeting with officials from my embassy. In reality, they wanted the information, but not to give such a meeting, and pretended afterward that I had simply agreed to write things down. They assumed I'd be a pushover. When it became clear on day three or four that I wasn't doing it, instead using the paper and pen they had given me to write, in the tiniest possible size, random thoughts, names of songs that popped into my head, little in-jokes between me and my girlfriend, things escalated. It came to midnight and I started dozing off, but the two guards who were always in the cell, always two of them, with five or six teams working in non-stop six-hour shifts, would scream at me to wake up and write. No sleep until I had written everything down. I called on their superior. A woman in her 40s or 50s. She had been present during the raid of my house, and also later when, after 24 hours, they technically moved me from being detained to being placed in RSDL.

She was not pleased when she arrived with an entourage of guards, translators and of course, Mr. Liu. I told her refusing me uninterrupted sleep constituted torture under the convention against torture. Maybe not the kind of torture people think of when they hear the word, but torture nonetheless. The convention against torture is one of few human rights treatises that China have actually ratified. She was teeming. How dare I? How can I be so disrespectful? Don't I realize how well they are treating me? It is true, they did treat me well, in comparison to most people in RSDL. In fact, few people ever see the inside of an RSDL facility without suffering severe mental- and physical torture. But, in the end, it worked. She instructed the guards to let me sleep. The next day, Mr. Liu no longer led most interrogations, his role having been spent by overplaying his hand, and "good cop" Zhang would take over.

--

The initial accusations against me had all been dispelled. They wanted to end this. My medical condition—Addison's disease, which could be fatal—offered them a way out. It was only later that they had begun to realize how serious this condition is, and that things could spiral out of control real quick. They wouldn't want a dead foreigner on their hands.

Towards the end of about two weeks of non-stop interrogations, having worn me down enough, with no sunlight, and fluorescent lights on 24/7, with nightly interrogation sessions to make sure I never had proper sleep, they had come to the realization that they had been wrong, I had been partially set up by someone else, as a way for that person to protect himself. This is not to say they didn't want to crush our work, and that the work would have been enough for them to go after us, but the specifics they gave for having detained me seemed to have all been dispelled.

Before any forced TV confession, however, they seem to have decided they needed a final test. I had come into this well prepared. I had read numerous accounts of people's interrogations, detentions, and torture. Something like this, being taken, had almost happened many times before. I and other all had drills to run when something was about to go down. I knew what my strategy was. Through this, I managed quite well. There is no right to remain silent of course. Instead, I had to know how to answer things, what could be said (and for believability *should* be said), but also what I could not. I also had to remember that many coworkers and partners were inside, and no one, no matter what, can ever follow things just like they planned. Things would come out.

On top of that, they were running data forensics on my computer, hard drives, USB sticks and more. Sure, they were all protected and encrypted, but file recovery can always find old deleted documents, or at least parts of them. Almost every day they would walk in with new papers in their hands, part of an excel sheet, a few pages of a document.

As long as I offered no direct lies, nothing that could be contradicted, I could still protect myself, and others. I painted a very wide and broad frame, with as little details as possible. After all, I was simply an administrator, a foreigner with limited Chinese, how could I possibly know the details on spending, on locations, names, participants. Most of what I could give was an empty frame. The basics. Without enough information to really compromise other people's safety. With this in mind, *the big test* would decide if all that would come crashing down like a house of cards, or be the final part convincing them that I was cooperating and that there was no reason for keeping me, nor my girlfriend, anymore.

"Several cameras were trained on my pupils, and a man attached electrodes to my fingers"

Would you mind doing a "psychological test" to "enhance our communication" the good cop asked me during a "fireside chat"? A bland Nescafe was given, along with the guards being told to put a pack of cigarettes on the table and let me smoke freely. Later that afternoon, after being led to the interrogation room, it would begin. As always, I was strapped to a wooden tiger chair. Uncomfortable to say the least, especially when being much taller than those it had been designed for. But, it was how you were seated for any interrogation. In this case, the room filled up, and besides the regular trio who would always sit behind a bench opposite me - the interrogation leader, the official responsible for taking notes, and the token translator - several others would join. The boss was there, but also two technicians.

A computer and various technical gadgets were standing in the middle of the room, in front of me. Several cameras were trained on my pupils, and a man attached electrodes to my fingers. It was a lie detector test. This session, like most, would go on for five or six hours. Test questions would be mixed with questions from the past, repeated again and again. My fingers would become sweaty, and they had to reattach the electrodes repeatedly. In the end, either my pupils didn't give me away, or they concluded the test didn't work. It wouldn't be done again, and I believe they now decided I could be trusted, they could believe my story. In a sense, it was the final test and end to their investigation of me. The rest, including the TV confession, was just about how they could use me before getting rid of me.

--

Every once in a while, Agent Zhang would visit me in my cell for these informal "fireside chats" instead of questioning me in the interrogation room. Often, a Nescafé would be offered, and he would bring a pack of cigarettes and I could smoke as much as I wanted. The heavy curtains would be opened for a bit of sunset light, or if it was night-time, the windows were opened for some fresh air. These were our "bonding" moments. Or rather, it was their way to create a sense of dependency in me for the "good cop" so that they could more easily persuade me to cooperate.

The previous night, I'd been woken at around three in the morning, hurried into the interrogation room opposite my cell, where for hours they had conducted a formal deposition. It would be my last time undergoing an interrogation session in that room. Earlier a cigarette had been given to me while one of the officers had a toilet break. "This is a first" agent Zhang told me, "the first time anyone has ever been allowed to smoke in here". A bit of history in the making I thought. Yet another small part to create a connection with the "good cop", a dependency.

Agent Zhang was now saying he needed something more to convince the judges not to prosecute. My written self-criticisms had not been enough. "I want to record a video of you accepting responsibility and showing that you know what you did was wrong," he said. The judges might be convinced by a video.

Up until this point they had spent a lot of time getting me to write self-criticisms. These were not about admitting any particular crime, but to admit to general wrongdoing. I was to put in writing, I now realized, that I had been wrong, that I had hurt China. Like Winston Smith, the protagonist in George Orwell's novel, *1984*, I was supposed to realize my wrongdoing, accept being reformed by the "helpful" State Security who had shown me the error of my ways, and to demonstrate that I actually believed it all. It wasn't an easy task.

At this point, I assumed, unlike earlier, although I was far from certain, that I would not be prosecuted, and that they were looking to find a way out. The media storm about my case had broken just a few days earlier—that much was made clear when they angrily asked about my relationship to the Reuters reporter Megha Rajagopalan who first broke my story, and who happened to be a friend of mine. Their anger about Michael Caster, my co-worker, who was handling advocacy and press on my behalf, was also clear. "He is spreading lies," they would yell. "What he is doing is hurting you." My casual remark that a phone call could fix all that did not go down well.

I said yes, sure, we can do that. Agent Zhang stood up and said he had to arrange some things and would be back shortly. He told me he would inform the guards that I could have a shower. He also left me the pack of cigarettes and said he would instruct the guards to give me more Nescafé if I wanted. He told me to put on my own clothes after my shower, instead of what I wore every day—grey sweatpants and sweater, with a fire-orange vest on top, all to make sure I felt like a criminal. He also told me I could shave if I wanted, but decided against it, why help them by making myself look better I thought.

"I have hurt the feelings of the Chinese people"

Not long after, maybe an hour or so later, he came back. He had brought his translator with him, which was rather comical because her English was no match for Agent Zhang's fluent grasp of the language.

Agent Zhang handed me a piece of paper with handwriting on both sides. He told me it was a "summary" of what had been said before during my endless interrogations and last night's deposition, but actually, it was a list of questions and answers, and I was to be one of two "actors" playing out a scene. I quickly scanned the page and the true nature of this recording became clear. I had to say: "I have hurt the feelings of the Chinese people." I became suspicious of the purpose of the recording, and that it might be for public use became clear— although no one admitted it—when later I was taken to the larger "meeting room" next to the interrogation room and saw the CCTV journalist and cameraman.

These TV confessions have not only become common now, but also much reported on, especially with more foreigners being forced to do them, and many rights defenders, especially lawyers, being forced to do them. However, by the time I was taken it had been rare enough that it didn't strike me as obvious at first. Most of the lawyers had at that point not been forced to make these, so sure, it existed, I knew about it, but it wasn't common enough for me to assume I was about to do it too. Until I meet and saw the CCTV journalist and cameraman that is.

But I still went along with it. I knew for sure that including that incredibly crass line about "hurt feelings" also meant that the media frenzy would go into overdrive. Everything else they wanted me to say would be negated by that one line. I might as well say: "I'm being forced to do this against my will, and no one has any reason to believe any of this is true."

Arguments followed. As always, they tried to subtly change my meaning or wording. During interrogations, we had had several shouting matches when both of us found our patience had run thin. The key issue was they insisted on calling lawyer Wang Quanzhang (王全璋) and other former partners "criminals," even though none of them had been convicted of any crime. I refused point blank. "There is simply no way I will call them criminals," I told them, "even semantically it doesn't make sense". "How can you be a criminal without a criminal conviction?" They relented.

Agent Zhang then left again, saying that he'd be back soon. "Please study the answers and memorize them," he told me. He returned with two guards in tow. They led me out of the cell across the narrow hallway to the "meeting room" where the recording was to be made. The room was packed. Agents Zhang and Liu (the "bad cop"), their supervisor, several young translators, the journalist, the cameraman, the officer who always handled taking notes, as well as several guards were all there. A small chair was reserved for me along the wall. Opposite, but outside of view from the camera, sat the female journalist, holding a piece of paper with the questions State Security had instructed her to read. She knew as well as me she was to be an actor, reading the lines as instructed by "director" Agent Zhang.

The journalist introduced herself. Confident. Fashionably dressed. Pretty. In her late 30s or early 40s. I was offered another cup of bland Nescafé. Behind us, one of the agents was holding a handheld camera. They discussed amongst themselves for a while, taking the paper from me and making small changes.

"Ok, let's go," the "bad cop" finally said.

"I knew I was about to become part of a pop-cultural phenomenon"

We ran through the seven or eight questions. A few retakes. Sit straighter they would say. Speak slower here. Change this here. Guidance. In between takes, the main "director" and "screenwriter" Agent Zhang discussed changes with the "bad cop" and their superior. Additional changes and re-takes followed. Once in a while, after scribbling changes, they handed me the paper so I could learn my new "lines." Once, I placed it down on the floor beside me before shooting resumed, but Agent Zhang spotted what I was trying to do and nabbed it, making sure it wouldn't be in the shot.

Most questions went well. I stumbled four times on the only line I really wanted to say: "I have hurt the feelings of the Chinese people." After the fourth take, the journalist leaned in and said: "You really don't want to say this line do you?" She couldn't have been more wrong. I nailed it on the fifth.

With that line, I knew I was about to become part of a pop-cultural phenomenon. A star, or perhaps more likely, an infamous villain.

I was led out, back to my cell, but told to keep my own clothes on. They came back and fetched me two more times to record some minor additions here and there. It was all done by 11. Agent Zhang seemed pleased.

--

Was it embarrassing? Were you hurt? Do you regret it? These are common questions from friends and journalists. Or, why did you do it? It's hard to answer these questions because when you do it makes it sound like you're trying to rationalize why you did it. For me, however, it was never really an issue. I had selfish reasons, such as I wanted to speed up my release, and the media frenzy I knew would come after being forced to say, "I have hurt the feelings of the Chinese people" would help with that. Every day I was being held mattered in terms of my medical condition. Other motives were nobler. I was repeatedly told that my girlfriend would only be released once my case had been dealt with, either by some form of release or being moved into pre-trial detention. They kept reminding me of this. Once, they showed me a photocopy of a drawing she had been allowed to make. It was devastating. That, and when they told me later she was being freed, were the only two times I almost cracked, but in the end, I managed to keep my tears in.

Because I didn't have to say anything of substance in that confession, and because I didn't have to denounce others, meant that the only thing left is the embarrassment of it all, a small price to pay for my girlfriend's and my own freedom. I also wanted badly to continue my rights work, and that was more important than being some kind of martyr. Unfortunately, what I didn't know at the time, was that the attack on my organization had been so wide-ranging that the NGO that I had run for so many years had to be dismantled.

Perhaps the most disturbing aspect was not seeing myself on TV but seeing colleagues. I knew their treatment must have been far worse than mine, I had to listen to one being beaten severely on the floor above me at one point, but seeing them on TV denouncing me continues to be a disturbing watch – even though they did the right thing, and I would never have wanted them to refuse. Frankly, I think the consequence for them, even with their faces blurred in the broadcast, has been far worse than for me, as they have reputations to consider. Unlike many other victims of forced televised confessions, I've always operated behind the scenes. Few people were aware of what I did, so I had no public reputation that could be destroyed. Still, it's embarrassing to be paraded on national television in front of hundreds of millions of viewers, and to this day, more or less every week, my name pops up in the news somewhere, and it's usually connected to that forced televised confession.

EPILOGUE

Rumors of Peter's imminent deportation began circulating in Beijing's diplomatic community a few days before it happened, and in the afternoon of January 26, he was taken, blindfolded, in a four or five car escort to Beijing airport, straight through the special diplomatic access area onto the tarmac and led onboard an SAS flight back to Sweden. He was officially deported under the then relatively new Espionage Act, banning him from entering China until 2026, and told that if he appears on Chinese soil the prosecution against him under article 107, using foreign funding to support activities endangering Chinese national security, will resume. The deportation order itself was illegal, as so many other steps taken during the judicial process against him.

Shortly after being released, his girlfriend, who had likewise been kept in 'residential surveillance at a designated location' for the same time he was kept, was allowed to leave China and reunite with Peter, where they settled in Thailand for a period to recuperate and decide how to move forward.

After dismantling "China Action" and taking steps to secure former partners and staff, Peter founded Safeguard Defenders, a China-focused human rights NGO, and Peter relocated to the safety of Europe.

Wang Quanzhang, Peter's original partner, remains missing, now for more than 1000 days.

TRIAL BY MEDIA
China's new show trials, and the global expansion of Chinese media

Chapter 6

Lawyer WANG YU

PROLOGUE

Wang Yu (王宇) is one of China's most respected human rights lawyers and one of its few female practitioners. Ironically, it was her own experience with the injustices of the Chinese legal system that turned her on that path.

Since then she has worked tirelessly representing the persecuted including moderate Uighur scholar Ilham Tohti (who is now serving life on conviction of separatism), a group of elementary school girls who had been sexually abused by their school principal (the story is the subject of the documentary *Hooligan Sparrow*), and the Feminist Five (a group of women protesting about sexual harassment).

However, in the summer of 2015, the Chinese Communist Party began mass arrests of rights lawyers and activists, now known as the 709 crackdown, whose main but not sole target was the Feng Rui Law Firm, her employer. She was one of the first to be taken. At 4am on the morning of 9 July, Beijing Security Bureau stormed into her apartment, using a power drill to break down her door. Ms. Wang, who was alone at the time, sent off a last frantic message to a Telegram group before she was flung onto her bed and handcuffed.

Wang would go on to spend the next 13 months under Residential Surveillance at a Designated Location and in detention, enduring physical and mental torture.

Wang Yu

It was the end of July 2015. I had been taken less than a month earlier, and my interrogator—he said his name was "Chief Wang"—started trying to convince me to go on television. I refused without a second's thought. I would not write anything and would never go on their television to confess.

On 1 August 2015, after dinner, a girl came in and told me to change my clothes. She said we had to go out for something. I asked: "Where? And for what?" She didn't know. She was just a messenger.

Chief Wang came into my cell after I had changed. He said he was taking me for my television confession. I was very angry. "I told you I would not record anything or go on television!" I said.

He didn't care. He just put a black hood over my head and, at least this time, he took me without putting me in handcuffs. In the car, I demanded again and again to be taken back. I told them I definitely wouldn't go on television. If they wanted to force me, I threatened to jump out of the car. Chief Wang maliciously told me to go ahead.

Of course, I just wanted to show my determination. I didn't want to die. I wanted to live for many more years.

We were in the car for more than an hour before reaching the CCTV building. They took me into the elevator. I kept repeating: "I won't record anything!"

"...it is okay. We will wait until you want to speak."

Once we got inside I was afraid that they would take me directly into the studio, and that they would be filming as soon as they took off my black hood. So, I put my head down and used my hair to cover my face once they removed the black hood.

I kept repeating: "I won't record anything!"

A person by the door said: "I heard your accent. Lawyer Wang is from Dongbei [northeast China]. I'm also from Dongbei; let's talk." I said I didn't know him and had nothing to talk to him about. Another person brought a bottle of water for me, asked me if I was thirsty and that we could talk after having some water. I was really quite thirsty, but I told him to stay away from me.

"I don't want to say anything! If you continue forcing me, I will kill myself right here."

In the end, a female host said: "If she really doesn't want to speak, let it go. Just let her leave."

Then she addressed me: "Lawyer Wang, I respect your determination. If you don't want to speak today, it is okay. We will wait until you want to speak."

"You have kidnapped me and are forcing me and violating my right to privacy. You don't need to wait. If you do, you will be disappointed. I will never come back here."

On our way out, no one spoke, but because I hadn't made a televised recording, I was so happy inside.

After a few days, maybe on 4 or 5 August, Chief Wang came back. He took me into a room like a hotel, but obviously we hadn't left the yard. The room was decorated like a standard hotel room. There was a bathroom with a normal door. Towards the back was a table, in front of which was a blue armchair. There was a single bed. The room was not big, about $10m^2$.

Chief Wang brought a camera with him this time. He still wanted me to reflect on my situation. I glared at him, saying nothing. I sat there the whole morning.

At around noon, Chief Wang disappointedly sent me back to the detention area.

On the morning of 7 August, the team leader took me to the so-called Beijing Tongda Guesthouse. We could hear the sound of airplanes in the sky every day. In the beginning, I thought we were near one of the airports, but afterwards I learned from a base manager that it was the same location as my previous detention facility, on the edge of Beijing, inside a military base, in a small town in Hebei Province.

That day, Chief Wang came to tell me that the crime I was officially now suspected of was "inciting subversion of state power" and so they had changed my coercive measure to Residential Surveillance at a Designated Location (RSDL).

I was speechless.

After I was transferred to Tianjin RSDL on 8 September 2015, my interrogators in Tianjin also tried to persuade me many times to go on television. I also refused.

The text under the photo said: Suspect Bao Zhuoxuan. I fainted immediately.

It was midnight, 10 October 2015. I had just fallen asleep when one of my guards woke me up and said the interrogators were coming soon. Two interrogators came in just after I had put on my clothes. They looked very serious. We all sat down and then they handed me two pieces of paper. I saw that the first piece was a telegram from Yunnan police department to the Inner Mongolia police department. It said that they had caught several people trying to smuggle across the border in Yunnan. One was Bao Zhuoxuan, aged 16, from Inner Mongolia and a student in Ulanhot [her son]. On the second page, suddenly, I saw a large photo of my son. It was the same kind of photo that gets taken when you first enter a detention center. He was stood against the wall with a height rule. The text under the photo said: Suspect Bao Zhuoxuan. I fainted immediately. I don't know how long I was unconscious, but when I woke up I was in bed and surrounded by several medical personnel. I still felt dizzy and was finding it hard to breathe. They told me my blood pressure was too high, gave me some medicine and then left.

My interrogator arrived. He told me that my son had been taken by anti-China forces but that luckily the police had found him and he was currently in Yunnan. He said my attitude would decide whether my son would be saved. I didn't know what to feel. I asked: how could I save him?

He said that I should record a video for the PSB boss to demonstrate my [good] attitude. I asked: What kind of video? What kind of attitude? They wrote down everything that I had to say on a piece of paper asked me to memorize it. I don't remember clearly what it said just that it was about denouncing certain anti-China forces.

Then they turned on the computer camera which was used during interrogations. They said: "Look you can see that we're not putting you on television, if we were, we would be using a professional camera". Two days later they told me the boss was happy with the recording and that my son was already in Ulanhot. This was how my first televised interview happened. I did not know at the time that it would be put on television, it wasn't until I was released and allowed to go back to Ulanhot, that my parents and my friends told me about it. [The police] broke their promise about not putting it on television.

--

It is difficult to explain, why I went on television, what kind of mental process I had gone through. And until now, I still feel it is difficult to describe, I don't know how to talk about it. **Actually, I do want to talk about it in detail, but I always feel sad. I am still struggling to get over the trauma. But I know I should speak out, even if just in this simple way.**

It was about April 2016 and I had already been transferred to the Tianjin First Detention Centre. I had just finished my breast surgery at that time and the guards and interrogators were taking quite good care of me.

The guard who was in charge of my cell would take me outside of the cell for a chat, or bring me something I otherwise could never get to eat. Humans are really strange animals. In fact, when I look back at it today, being able to eat and move around are the most basic of rights – but because I ate bad food, was mistreated, etc. – just a little bit of warmness, just a slight improvement in the situation, and all the sudden you feel grateful. Maybe this is Stockholm syndrome? But in fact, the most unbearable thing I had in the detention center was that every time I went in and out of the cell, I had to take off all my clothes and then turn around. This was really the most painful thing for me. I actually raised it with the guard who was in charge of my cell many times. That system should be changed, but of course it is impossible. It's really painful to endure such torture every day!

My interrogator said if I cooperated then my case would be "dealt with leniently." He meant I could be released soon. Those days, they stopped using words like "we will take Bao Longjun and Bao Zhuoxuan tomorrow" to threaten me. Of course, at that time I already knew that my husband was taken too. They also kept reminding me that my dream of sending my son overseas to study could happen only once I had been released from the detention center.

How, then, did they want me to cooperate? They said all the 709 Crackdown people need to demonstrate a good attitude before they would be dealt with leniently. They said a PSB boss would come to the detention center in a few days and they wanted me to say to him that: "I understand my mistake, I was tricked, and I was used. I denounce those overseas anti-China forces and I am grateful for how the PSB have helped and educated me." After that, they stopped taking me to the interrogation room and moved me to a staff office where they fixed up space for me to eat and memorize the material my interrogator gave me.

...with the script typed into the computer in a huge font size.

Around about the end of April, the interrogator told me the boss was coming today and that we should make the video. He promised me the video would only be shown to that boss, and it would definitely not be shown to the public. He told me not to worry and just follow the script they had given to me. If I couldn't memorize it all, then we could just re-record it. They also told me that everyone who was caught up in the 709 Crackdown had already make such a video. I kept asking them to confirm that it wouldn't be shown in public and they promised that it would not. Despite their assurances, I was still very unhappy about having to do the video.

In the afternoon, I was taken to the office again. A few minutes later, a man came in; he was in plainclothes and about 50 years old. A young man in his 20s followed with a camera. They both said something similar to me; something about how they would find a way out for me. I have suffered a lot of memory loss in the past few years so even if I try to remember exactly what happened, I can't. But I do remember asking him who would see the video and he repeatedly said that it was only for their boss and not for television.

The young man finished setting up the camera, then the older one started asking questions. I don't remember the exact questions, but it was basically the same as my interrogator had told me to study. I didn't answer very well, because my memory was bad and also I didn't want to make the video. I really messed up some of the questions and they had to ask me again and again. After three or four hours, they eventually left.

Some 20 days later, I heard that the so-called PSB boss had said that last video was not good enough and that we had to record it again. So, we recorded it again, but two days later, my interrogator said it still wasn't acceptable. **The next time they came with a camera and a computer, with the script typed into the computer in a huge font size. They wanted me to read it from the screen and look into the camera.** We recorded it like this many times and finally they left. But another two days later they came back and said it still wasn't good enough, so we did it all again. But that didn't pass either.

It was about the beginning of June, one day before the Dragon Boat festival, when my interrogator told me that another boss was coming and wanted to talk to me. If I behaved well I could get out of the detention center. Not long after, two men in their 50s or 60s in plainclothes, came in. They surprised me by shaking my hand when they first arrived. Later, I learned they were the vice-director and division chief of Tianjin PSB. They talked briefly about my health and my situation and then asked me to give a self-evaluation. I said: "Of course, I think that I am a good person and also a good lawyer. I believe in behaving with kindness and I am professional in my work and have always won my clients' approval."

After that they often took me to their office to talk with them. They kept trying to persuade me to do an interview on television, but I kept saying no.

In the beginning of July, my interrogator talked to me alone. He said, **"Think carefully. If you don't agree to go on television how will you be able to get out? How will your husband Bao Longjun be able to get out? How will your son ever be able to study abroad?"**

I thought hard about it for a few nights. I thought, neither me nor my husband can communicate with anyone from outside. Who knows when it will all end. And my poor son was home without us. We didn't know how he was doing. Although, my interrogator told me that he had been released and was living in Ulanhot, he might be under surveillance, he didn't have his parents with him. What kind of future would he have?

I though the two so-called "bosses" who had been talking with me looked like they would keep their word. After speaking with them for many days, I trusted them, and the people around me treated me much better. Much better than when I was in RSDL, where they were very cruel to me.

So, I decided to accept. I just wanted to see my son so much. I thought, if I couldn't get out my son would never be able to study overseas. I might get out many years later, but by then what would have happened to my son? If he was harmed now, the trauma would stay with him his whole life. I needed to be with him during this stage of his life. I decided that I would do my best to help my son go to a free country and study. He would no longer live like a slave, suffering in this country. He has to leave, he must leave, I thought. That was the most urgent thing. **So I had to do it, even if it meant doing something awful.**

I also considered the possibility that they might break their promise—and if they did I vowed to fight. So, I said yes to their request to go on television, but only if they released me first. **I started practicing the script they prepared for me and we rehearsed it many times, almost every day before I left the detention center.**

On 22 July 2016, they went through the formality of my "release on bail." They took me from the Tianjin First Detention Centre to the Tianjin Police Training Base under Tianjin Panshan Mountain. I stayed there for about 10 days.

They transferred me to Tianjin Heping Hotel and for the next two days I was still under their control. I did the interview in a western-style building near the Heping Hotel a few days later. That afternoon, about 4 or 5pm I was reunited with my son. He hugged me and cried for a long time. I also quietly shed tears.

The next day, my son and I met his father Bao Longjun who had also just been released on bail.

After my release I became very depressed. We were kept under house arrest in Ulanhot. My son and his father often made fun of me because of what I had said on that television interview and I felt very hurt and under a lot of pressure. One time, when I couldn't stand it anymore, I asked my son, "Would you rather I suffered and went on television so I could be with you, or would you prefer that I didn't go on television but then stayed in prison?" My son said emphatically: "I want my mum with me!"

Hearing my son say this, I believe that everything I suffered was worth it. This was the only way I could be reunited with my son, so I had to do it.

When I got back home, I gradually began to understand what kind of pain my son had been through over the past year. Such cruelty caused my son to suffer from severe depression and that made me even more determined to settle my son overseas so that he could heal both mentally and physically.

So, this is my story. I don't expect everyone to understand. I just want to say that my son is everything to me. Perhaps, I had no other choice.

EPILOGUE

Since her release on bail, 13 months after being taken, she has been one of the few 709 victims to speak openly, including on what happened after her time inside.

After I was released on bail, our whole family was exiled to Inner Mongolia. State security rented an apartment for the three of us. They occupied the apartment opposite ours, so they could watch us 24/7.

My son has never talked about it with me in detail. It was only through fragmentary words with my son, both sets of grandparents, and aunts, that I have learned a bit about what happened to him.

Every morning two or three police would take my son to school; [and] would bring him back in the evening. There were three cameras pointed at him in his classroom, as well as cameras in the school corridors, and even a special monitoring room at the school. State security officers patrolled the school.

[I later learned that] they made my son frame other people. They told him exactly what he had to say. He didn't agree, so they hit him, with a thick, long wooden staff. They started at him in the lower back, moving higher and higher, smashing it into his back, while yelling: "If you don't write what we say, we're going to go all the way up to your head and smash your skull in." My son begged for their forgiveness, responding: "Don't hit me, it hurts too much, I can't take it anymore; just write what you want and I'll sign it, isn't that enough?"[1]

TRIAL BY MEDIA
China's new show trials, and the global expansion of Chinese media

Chapter 7

Fraud Investigator **PETER HUMPHREY**

PROLOGUE

Peter Humphrey (彼特・威廉・汉弗莱), a British citizen, former journalist and long-term resident of China, was running a corporate due diligence firm, ChinaWhys, when he was detained along with his wife in July 2013. Police accused his firm of illegally obtaining Chinese citizens' personal information, but it is widely believed that he was targeted because of his investigative work for pharmaceutical giant GlaxoSmithKline (GSK), which was at that time embroiled in a corruption scandal. GSK had hired ChinaWhys earlier that year to probe the background of a suspected whistleblower. Mr. Humphrey unwittingly became a victim in a much larger high stakes game with issues ranging from corruption and prostitution to corporate espionage.

Indeed, the very first high-profile televised confession broadcast that same month, was of Liang Hong, a Chinese citizen and senior executive of GSK's China operations. Weeks later, Peter Humphrey too was being paraded on TV in an orange prison vest. He would go on to be paraded on national TV not once but twice, first in August 2013 soon after his detention, and again a year later in July 2014, after his indictment and shortly before his sham trial.

On both occasions, they also coerced his wife, Ms. Yu Yingzeng[3] (Ying), an American citizen, to be filmed making false confessions.

---

[3] Surname Yu, official personal name Yingzeng, short name Ying.

Up until being hired by GSK, my company ChinaWhys had performed some 700 corporate due diligence and anti-fraud investigations. Running ChinaWhys and performing corporate due diligence was what I did for a living, and it had been for a long time. I started in this field back in the late 1990s, after having worked as a reporter and editor for Reuters in Eastern Europe, the Balkans and Hong Kong.

Even though our main office was in Shanghai, I and my wife Ying lived in Beijing. China had been our family home for almost 20 years by this time. Our son, who had just turned 18, knew no other home than our home in Beijing. He had just left for Hong Kong to start an internship when this all started.

This all began with our investigation on behalf of GSK. In April 2013 GSK approached ChinaWhys and hired us specifically to investigate the background of a former executive of GSK. She had been pushed out of the company, and GSK believed she was seeking revenge by smearing the company. She had earlier managed relations for GSK with the Chinese government. We were also tasked to conduct a security assessment on the apartment of GSK's China country manager, a British citizen named Mark Reilly. He had been covertly filmed in his apartment having sex with a Chinese woman, and the video had been sent to GSK's board. The fact that GSK had indeed been involved in bribery and was being investigated by the Chinese police, the PSB, was kept hidden from us. With this, we were on a collision course with the PSB.

We submitted our report to GSK on 6 June that year, and two or three weeks later the PSB raided GSK offices and detained GSK managers across China. I was informed that the executive whom we were hired to investigate had seen our report and was going to retaliate against us. On July 10, our office was raided, and both I and my wife Ying were seized.

--

We were both taken to and held in the Shanghai Number 1 Municipal Detention Centre. After a day-long interrogation in a subterranean cell in the belly of the Shanghai PSB headquarters, the notorious "building 803", I was tossed into a cell with 12 other detainees in the middle of the night. The detention center cell was a small unfurnished cell, some 15 sqm for 13 cellmates. I did not know it at the time but this would be my home for 14 months. We slept on the hard floor, with the ceiling light always on. There would be no letter writing or phone calls for a long time. My interrogation, and subsequent televised "confessions" would all take place over the 14 months I lived there. My wife Ying was in a separate cell two floors up in a wing for female prisoners. Her conditions were similar to my own.

--

It was a Saturday, August 24, the day after Ying's birthday. I was summoned to an interrogation by two of my police interrogators. This was most unusual, you know, because they never used to come on Saturdays. The fact that they came on a Saturday suggests there was some kind of emergency; they'd been ordered to come...

"...our bosses want you to 'meet the media'"

They had come to proposition me or ask me to do this media interview. The officer who presented this to me was one of the two lead interrogators who had questioned me over the preceding six or seven weeks. It was Chief Inspector Ding Zhidong from the Third Brigade of the Shanghai Criminal Investigation Department. He was the one who played the "good cop" role in my interrogations. There was another one who played the "bad cop" role, Chief Inspector Bao, who was not here this day. The guy who came to propose this, Ding, was accompanied by another police officer whose name was Huang Xin, who played a secondary role in my interrogations. These two guys were the same two guys who had raided our house in Beijing, while the other officers were raiding our office in Shanghai on 10 July.

Officer Ding said to me: "Peter, there's been a lot of media coverage on your case, and our bosses want you to 'meet the media,'" and so we discussed this a bit. I was uncomfortable with the whole idea, knowing what the Chinese propaganda machine was like. So, I asked who would it be, how many would it be, what kind of media would it be, and so on. They said they wanted to take pictures, and film it and I said I can't accept that. They said we can blur your image, but I said I don't want any film, any images at all. I'm willing to meet two or three print journalists. At the end of this short meeting, they asked if I would write a line or two to show I agreed. I wrote that I agreed to meet several print journalists, no pictures, no filming. And I signed that.

At this point, I had been locked up for six or seven weeks, with very poor and dirty nutrition, no outdoor exercise or sunshine, no proper bathing facilities, lights on 24/7, no medical care, almost daily interrogations in handcuffs locked in a metal chair and cage.

I wasn't comfortable with doing it at all. But when you're in that situation, you've been under duress for such a long time, if something appears that it might possibly be a lifeline, or half a lifeline, or a means to mitigate circumstances, then you clutch at it. But I certainly did not accept the concept of a lot of journalists, cameramen, I did not accept it, I made that very clear and I wrote it down.

I was resisting the idea altogether but they said if I cooperated it would mean more lenient treatment or "we would view your case more favorably", which of course turned out to be completely untrue.

--

I was suffering a lot from physical pain because I had a whiplash injury of some sort from when the police raided us and kicked the door into my face. It had injured my neck and my back and I was in a lot of pain.

But medical treatment was withheld. This denial of treatment would become far worse later in my captivity when I developed cancer, for which treatment was also withheld. Later, it would take several years of investigation and treatment to beat my cancer after I was released. Of course, in captivity I also had a lot of anxiety, panic attacks and so on, and sleeplessness, and so I had managed to persuade them to give me a sleeping pill from time to time, but they only gave me a tiny dose.

On that Monday morning, the doctor who patrolled the detention center, who was a civilian contractor, came and gave me a sedative, which he said was to calm me down. And I took it. I would take anything that would help to calm me down. This one made me very dopey. That was totally unusual because the sedative was usually only given in the evenings and it was usually nowhere near as strong.

Not long after that, they brought me a new prison vest, you know those orange prison vests and told me to change into it. I didn't know why. Usually, we were wearing very tatty, very filthy vests. It was unusual that someone got given a new one.

Shortly after that, they came and fetched me out of the cell. Normally, when you are taken out of your cell, you are taken out by one warden, who puts cuffs on you, but that day there were four or five. One of them had a video-camera. The detention center had its own 'propaganda department'. Sometimes the wardens would film things that would happen in the detention center. That morning, they were there to film me coming out of the cell door, I think. At that moment, though, I didn't really know why.

Our cell block had a long corridor…. Come out, turn left, cross an indoor bridge, which brings you to another block, with a door on either end. Since my release I have seen pictures from CCTV showing me being led down that corridor that morning in the prison vest, in cuffs and looking awful. When we went through the second door of the bridge, I was ambushed by a gang of people with cameras – I hesitate to say journalists — some of them had still cameras and some of them had video cameras.

So now I understood what was going on. This shocked me. It was clear they had not respected my wishes, even though they told me that they would. They had cheated me.

So, they led me down this corridor which was where I normally went for my interrogations. There are interrogation cells lining both sides of that corridor. I went further down the corridor than I had been before, to a room on the left which was a much larger interrogation cell than normal.

--

It was set up like a tribunal. There was a fairly large podium with a long bench and a number of officers sat behind it, including my other lead interrogator, who I referred to as bad cop, inspector Bao, his surname, and some senior officers whose names I did not know. Some of my warders stood in the doorway and watched.

Ding led the proceedings. He had a script in his hand.

In the center of the room was a cage with steel bars and inside the cage was a seat with a crossbar that locks across your lap. Chinese prisoners call it a tiger chair. I was in handcuffs and wearing this orange prison vest but I had not been convicted of any crime. I was made to sit in this locked chair in this steel cage and the gang of so-called journalists and quite a number of police officers basically surrounded it. These police officers included Ding, Bao, and another officer involved in our case called Lu Wei, who appears in some Chinese media footage about our case.

Ding led the proceedings. He had a script in his hand. The police officers were all in uniform for this occasion. Previously I had never seen them in uniform. Usually they wore civilian clothes.

So there I am, dopey, shocked, in handcuffs in a locked iron chair, inside a locked steel cage inside an interrogation cell surrounded by so-called journalists and police officers poking lenses through the gaps in the cage... I was totally surrounded, with spotlights and lenses poking through. It was quite a horrifying scene.

Then Ding basically read out questions from his script. I was very, very awkward, I was deliberately awkward and involuntarily awkward at one and the same time because of my physical and mental state. I was drugged and dopey. I was caged. What goes through your mind when you are sitting in a cage like that? What's going to happen next? It's like trying to balance on a tightrope. Trying to be reasonable but also not confessing to things you didn't do, which I was being pressured to do. It was very, very difficult. There was nowhere to run to.

I have flashbacks of this televised confession and it figures very high in my post-traumatic stress disorder [PTSD). It is one of these horror moments that often comes back to me and upsets me even now.

Ding's questions were all aimed at getting me to confess, to say I broke the law, to say yes I know I broke the law, I'm very sorry, forgive me, and so forth. I was not prepared to do that. I knew that I was innocent, I hadn't broken any law, the law was being bent to fit around me and incriminate me.

So, a lot of my responses during this cage interview were attempts to rebut any suggestion that we had violated the law.

The media were not allowed to ask questions. One of the cameramen had a movie camera with the CCTV name on it and he was together with a CCTV reporter, a woman.

My recollection is that I used language with conditionals in it, I was in this cage I was under duress I was being treated like a caged animal, not knowing when I would be let out, what I believe I said was along the lines: If I had violated the law and such and such that I did so unknowingly and I'm sorry. But there's no way that I ever said: "Yes I know I broke the law." The little clips that I've seen since my release are almost unrecognizable to me.

--

After the so-called interview, which they were going to call a confession, I felt totally humiliated and crushed.

Officer Ding escorted me back out to the end of that particular corridor. He put his arm over my shoulder and told me I had done well,

TRIAL BY MEDIA
China's new show trials, and the global expansion of Chinese media

I felt so disgusted. He knew that I was shaking, that I was angry, and I think he knew he had committed a crime against me.

I believe they deceptively edited everything I said that morning and added totally fabricated statistics that went into print.

I had absolutely no chance to see a lawyer beforehand to discuss whether or not to do the interview, and this was probably timed quite deliberately to make sure that I couldn't do that. This propaganda exercise was clearly intended to bolster the charges that were laid just a few days earlier and was to counter a wave of international media coverage on our case (which I had not yet seen).

It bears no semblance with reality. And the conditions in which this interview took place were nothing short of torture.

After the filming in the cage, I felt totally humiliated and crushed. I felt totally wronged. They had cheated me very explicitly; treated me like an animal... I realized then the significance of having given me that sedative. You feel helpless.

--

She [the CCTV journalist] didn't like what she was hearing. It was not what she wanted.

In the end, this was not going to be my only televised "confession". There would be another. Again on a Saturday, this time in July 2014, almost a year after the first one. While my detainees were washing their clothes in the sink and watching football on the cell's TV, I was summoned for interrogation. My cellmates were again mystified because this – along with some other events of the previous couple of days – was out of the ordinary for a detainee so close to his trial date, with the PSB investigation already supposedly closed.

But I was not led along the usual corridor route to the interrogation block this time. Instead a warder led me down to the yard and to the yard door of the interrogation block at its far end, normally used by PSB officers and visiting lawyers. There at the door stood one of my lead interrogators, officer Bao and one of his minions who I did not recognize. We did not enter. We talked in the doorway. "Hey, Peter, our bosses want you to meet the media," he said. I was surprised and yet not surprised. The last time I had 'met the media' I was conned and ambushed by cameramen and subjected to a fake media interview inside a steel cage conducted by my other lead interrogation officer, Ding Zhidong. On that occasion, they had dressed it up as a confession of crime, and churned out fake statistics about our business to make us look like information traffickers.

"What's the point?" I asked. "I don't want to do another 'meet the media'," I said. "This one will be different," Bao said. "You can say what you like," he said. "Can I talk about GSK?" I asked. 'Yes, you can," he said. But you filmed me in handcuffs in a cage," I protested. "If I meet the media again, I don't want to be treated like that. I don't want handcuffs and a cage, I want a normal setting." Bao said I could go to the encounter without cuffs and in an open room, and like a fool I agreed. I had no idea of the level of international media coverage we had been getting this month, and I did not realize that the authorities wanted to counter it with their own propaganda. "When will it be?" I asked. "After lunch," Bao said. They led me to the meeting room.

A group of about a dozen mostly youngish people in civilian clothes, male and female, were there. It was hard to know whether any of them were really journalists, or who among them was something else.

"Where are you all from?" I asked the gathering. There were China Central Television (CCTV), the *PSB Daily* and several other outfits whose names I had not heard of but sounded like propaganda organs of the judiciary or the police. "I am from CCTV," said one woman, in a white blouse, and she took the lead. She sat on a second chair facing me, and a CCTV cameraman wielding a TV camera began to film. She did not tell me her name.

"How are you being treated?" the CCTV journalist asked. "The detention center officers are kind to me, but the conditions here are very bad. I have many health problems," I said. "But you look okay to me," she said, taking sides. "I have a prostate condition that might be cancer, a hernia, spine problems and many other ailments. None of them have been treated properly," I said. She didn't like what she was hearing. It was not what she wanted.

"Tell us about your charge," she said. "You are charged with trafficking information," she said. "I am not charged with trafficking information," I said. "I am charged with illegally obtaining citizens' information, and I am not guilty of that charge," I said. She began lecturing me. "I don't approve," she said. She spoke to me with a hectoring tone of authority, not the tone of a journalist at all.

It was clear to me now these "journalists" had a well primed agenda set by the PSB. It was not going to do us any good at all. I shuddered inside myself to think how Ying might handle this if they also 'interviewed' her. Unbeknown to me at that time, they did indeed also record an interview with Ying, and the two were edited together and released before our trial started to skew public opinion. We saw some of this footage after our release, a year or so after this.

EPILOGUE

On August 8, 2014 Peter Humphrey was found guilty by a Chinese court and sentenced to two and a half years in prison in August 2014, shortly after his second televised appearance. Peter Humphrey has always insisted on his innocence and says Chinese officials denied him medical treatment for suspected prostate cancer while he was in prison, saying that he must first sign a written confession, which he refused to do.

In June 2015, under diplomatic pressure and his failing health, he and his wife were eventually released, in Peter's case seven months early, and deported from China.

In the UK after release, Peter Humphrey spent several years battling his untreated prostate cancer, and underwent treatment for post-traumatic stress disorder. He and his wife have launched a lawsuit against GSK for deceiving them, claiming it led to their imprisonment and all sorts of damages. They also filed a complaint to the central government in Beijing, which was ignored

Following their deportation, they lost their business, their assets in China, and both their incomes, while western banks closed or locked their accounts.

Peter Humphrey wrote a long and harrowing account of his experience in Chinese prisons which appeared in the Financial Times Magazine[4] on February 16, 2018. He is working on a book about justice and imprisonment in China.

---

[4] https://www.ft.com/content/db8b9e36-1119-11e8-940e-08320fc2a277

TRIAL BY MEDIA
China's new show trials, and the global expansion of Chinese media

Chapter 8

Lawyer **WEN QING**

PROLOGUE

Wen Qing (温清) is a lawyer in his mid-30s, and one of China's rights defense lawyers – a small group willing to defend those the Chinese state think should not be defended. Wen, originally a commercial-oriented lawyer from China's southwest, became involved in rights defense work gradually, having meet some other rights defense lawyers a few years after graduating and starting work.

Wen has undertaken a fair amount of "sensitive" cases, but is still young, and was in his mind targeted more as means to get information on others, and for his role working with other rights defenders in organizing, and often teaching at, training activities arranged in law, human rights and related issues.

Wen spent about a month inside China's feared system called "residential surveillance at a designated location", where police kept him, like all other RSDL victims, in solitary confinement. Wen is a rare case without physical torture, but was instead greatly humiliated, and used as a target to attack others, and denounce himself, in a way that would require a very long walk back to be able to work as a rights defender again, and for repairing his image.

A shorter excerpt from this, his full story, was presented in Safeguard Defenders report "Scripted and Staged".

TRIAL BY MEDIA
China's new show trials, and the global expansion of Chinese media

I knew it was happening, but when they burst into my apartment in the morning it was just as shocked as if I hadn't expected it. I never had my home raided, or taken away blindfolded before. Any problems I had have with police had been being forbidden to do this, being called in to discuss that, etc., and sure, I had been kept overnight before, but never been formally detained or arrested. I wasn't considered big fish enough for that I guess. Something had changed.

...someone stood behind the camera, holding up large note cards with my lines on them.

Over the last few months things had gotten hotter. The number of times I'd been invited to 'drink tea' with police had increased, and before the raid, higher and higher ups had become involved in these informal interrogations. It was clear it was heading to a show down, and I'd done what I could to prepare. It ended up that police had been a step ahead of me. Deleting documents, emails, cleaning computers and phones had all helped, but it seemed police had snuck into my house, made copies of my keys, while I was away on business during this time.

Not long ago I was supposed to meet another lawyer. Before doing so, police had called me up, again, asking me for a 'tea chat', the kind that you can't really say no to. I went, was kept all afternoon and night, not allowed to leave until the next day. By the time I was free the lawyer I was supposed to meet had already been disappeared. Now it was my turn.

Knowing it was coming had brought the level of nervousness to unbearable levels the few days before. I couldn't get anything done, couldn't focus. Even though it was nice of my friend to try to convince me the flee, to leave China, I didn't feel I had anywhere to go, and it just made me feel even worse. When they finally came the nervousness melted away and felt like my normal self again. The waiting was over.

--

I was never told that the recording would be televised. The police lied. Earlier, they had placed me in a secret prison. Now, weeks after being put into solitary confinement, they wanted me to agree to record a video, to show their "bosses." The point they made to me, repeatedly, was that a video would show that I was being cooperative, and that I had accepted that I had been wrong. It was commonly done in China and didn't raise an eyebrow at all. In fact, I would have been surprised had they not asked this, unless they were already certain they wanted to prosecute me. However, at this point, after weeks of daily and nightly interrogations, I was for from sure, but I suspected they didn't want to prosecute me. I assumed they would keep me, maybe for the full six months they are allowed, but probably try to scare me and then release me somehow. Making a video for their superiors made sense.

Mr. Bao, the friendlier of the two interrogators handling my case, came into my cell one afternoon and sat down for a talk. He wanted to help me he said. He needed my help to do that. He had to show his bosses that I was cooperating, and that he was right—that I should be released in some way, and not prosecuted. My friends and partners had made videos [colleagues or partners also taken into custody], Mr. Bao said. He showed me a transcript of what they had said, and although he did not give me enough time to read much of it, it was nonetheless clear: record the video, and you might get released. No video, no release.

After that nothing much happened. They had largely stopped the draining all night-long interrogations, and I sat trying to kill time in my cell, staring into the suicide-proofed padded walls for maybe three or four days before the actual recording happened. I should have known something was up because before the big production, Mr. Bao, with Mr. Yin, who always tried to be mean and threatening, and Mr. Wang, their superior, all came into my cell together with a group of guards. I was told I could shower, even wash my hair, and then put on the clothes I had worn when they detained me. Later, I was blind-folded and taken down into the basement car park. I have very little recollection of how long we drove, but it felt like a long time, I remember being stuck in traffic. By the time my blindfold was removed I was inside a large hotel suite. This is where I was to record the first of two videos, the video that would end up on national TV, against my knowledge. In the end I would learn about it from friends who would tell me, several days after I was partially released. However, a few days after making the second of the video, and while police were doing what turned out to be their last interrogations sessions, they would threaten me that the video be released if I didn't cooperate.

--

The forced TV confession was the last part.

It would begin with interrogations, many of them, every day or, more commonly, night. Perhaps the most extreme was the first three or four days, when they were nonstop, with no sleep in between. In fact the first 10 hours or so was spent strapped into a tiger chair with a hood over my head, just sitting there. The interrogators, there were several teams, would take turn and get their rest in between, while I was going into near unconsciousness towards the end. After three days

I was given a few tiny steamed buns. So small it didn't make a dent in my hunger, but I guess enough to keep me from losing consciousness.

The few weeks after that would be better, but the cold room, where I was forced to be naked in bed, along with guards regularly coming over to my small bed to lift the blanket, occasionally slap or punch my face, meant that I didn't really get proper sleep for about a month. By the time the recording of a video, not for TV, but for internal use for their superiors, got around I was a shell of myself.

This was my life, and now I could no longer work, and I could feel my reputation getting ruined day by day.

The only good part of being so drained was that I didn't have the energy nor time to really think about my treatment, my situation. If I wasn't strapped into the tiger chair, I was thinking about the interrogations, what had been said, what would come next.

They found their most effective tactic early on. They would casually ask me about my parents, their health. Would they survive this? What If I was sentenced and sent to prison for say 10 years. Would they be alive by the time I might be released? Did I realize my behavior with them now would largely determine how this would affect my parents? Examples were given, examples of other rights defenders whose parents had died while they were inside. I have to admit, such psychological tactics worked well on me.

--

After having arrived at the hotel suite looking room for making the video, they seated me on a chair by one of the walls. The curtains were all closed, and the door to the other room inside was closed. People, including the three investigators, entered and returned from behind that closed door. I assumed senior officers must be sitting there giving directions. A television camera on a large tripod was set up, and besides the cameraman, other police officers were walking around. The hotel was obviously a very expensive one, with that gaudy style officials and businessmen like. It looked bad, but also expensive.

Before I had been taken, there had been an increase in people, often lawyers, being forced to "confess" on TV, but it hadn't been used enough by that time to be that well known. Seeing the expensive camera and all the equipment however made me suspect that maybe this wasn't just an internal video, but something else. I didn't protest, in fact I said nothing. At this stage, I thought my release was more important.

Both interrogators who entered the room from the back were holding a piece of paper. I later realized this was the paper with my questions and answers, prepared for me to read into the camera. I had to learn them by heart. Later on, as we took breaks between takes they would add things or change what I was supposed to say. Once we actually started, they would not only decide what I was to say, but how I said it: the speed of my voice, the exact wording, the expression on my face. After they brought me a draft with the questions and answers and asked me to copy it by hand., It made me feel a little bit like a schoolboy, copying whole books as if that was the way to learn. Still, despite this ridiculous exercise, when we did start recording, someone stood behind the camera, holding up large note cards with my lines on them. The cameraman finished setting up the extra lighting, and we got going.

The whole thing was staged, prepared.

Mr. Bao read out the questions first. All of it was choreographed, and the whole thing went on perhaps seven hours, with so many retakes I can't remember for sure.

The production would go on a long time. Any mistake, we just had to do a retake. In the end, not just the words, but the speed of my speaking, the way I looked, my tone, everything had to be just so, before they were pleased enough that we could move on the next line or answer.

By the time we were getting close to the end I felt really unwell. I hadn't eaten. I am hypoglycemic and my blood sugar had gotten very low, too low. I felt dizzy, starting to sweat. One of my guards actually seemed a little nervous, and he brought me some fruit and yogurt. After a while, I felt a bit better.

In the end they didn't insist on me calling anyone a criminal and I would be largely just repeating what others had said in their videos, as far as I knew. One thing was made clear though, there was no room for bargaining. I was to say exactly, word for word, what they decided. There was no debate.

As we were recording, taking breaks, other agents or officers would fill up the room, but of course, you never see them on screen. It would be the middle of the evening by the time we returned to the prison, and as before the whole trip, from the hotel room to the cell, I was blindfolded.

After settling back into the prison after having made the video they didn't interrogate me. I asked for something to read, a newspaper or a book, anything to pass the time. They refused.

--

It would take several more days of killing time inside the cell before Mr. Bao came back. They wanted to make another video. Right away it seemed. This time the two guards in the cell led me across the small corridor into a larger room. My cell, the interrogation room, and this larger room, was my world when I was inside.

This time it was just the three interrogators. Mr. Bao lead the session, reading the questions for me. One of the others would hold a small handheld camera and record me. A paper, with questions and answers, were simply placed in front of me. They had written everything down for me, and I simply had to speak whatever was written. A very different experience from the expensive production before.

I never did understand why they wanted the second one. It was never used. Most of the questions were exactly the same. The only difference was they wanted me to admit being part of a human rights network. I admitted. In the end, they never used the recording.

--

It would be two or three days after my release that I saw the CCTV piece. I could read online about it, and people were talking about it on WeChat. Funnily, I didn't manage to find the actual video at first, only print reports, and had to use a VPN to circumvent China's firewall.

The way they chose [what I had to say] and edited [the confession recording] made me incredibly upset. I was so damn angry. Worse, it ruined my reputation among many people. Some people thought I had sold out friends and partners. Ever since my reputation has taken a big hit, and some pretty mean things have been said by people who have no idea what they are talking about, or the fact that [it was faked and edited]. If you read what I said, you realize that I didn't really say anything about [those people] but that's the impression people get watching the whole shit piece anyway.

The police had told me, repeatedly, how well they had treated me, and that compared to other lawyers. It is true, reading about other lawyers testimony or talking with others who were placed in RSDL I seem to be one of the few that wasn't subjected to physical torture – no one beat me or tried to use physical pain to force me. Still, once I was finally out after being in solitary confinement for a month, I felt both physically and mentally destroyed. The almost constant lack of sleep over a month had left my body weaker than I could have imagined.

In the end, I was only released on bail. It would be a year of living under supervision, and with severe restrictions. It would take a while before I got to see my own TV appearance, and having seen it, and having been told online by others that I had appeared on TV was made worse by the simple fact that I couldn't address it. I couldn't retract it, or post an explanation, or anything. If I did, they would just say I violated by bail, and take me again. Worse still, for many month I could not only not work, but wasn't even allowed to have dinner or lunch with people. I was forced into isolation, and couldn't even share my thoughts with a friend. All the while I knew more and more people were learning about my "confession".

I'd been a lawyer for almost ten years when this happened, and been involved in "rights defense cases" for more than five. This was my life, and now I could no longer work, and I could feel my reputation getting ruined day by day. The anger at the police, not just all of them but the individual officers, who had lied about the video, and what it was for, just kept growing.

I was stranded and stuck. A police man lived near my house in my mom's hometown, the only place I was allowed to live. Weekly meetings, besides informal visit by the neighboring police, along with knowing my phone was monitored, meant I could barely for anything.

TRIAL BY MEDIA
China's new show trials, and the global expansion of Chinese media

EPILOGUE

Wen chuckled when saying that he couldn't find his own forced TV confession to view at first after having been released – he had to use a VPN to leap over the Great Firewall to find somewhere to view it.

After viewing it, and realizing the damage it would undoubtedly have done to his reputation, he was despondent, without being able to see any way out. He had been released on bail, meaning he would live under tight surveillance for a year, and even the slightest act to aggravate the police meant he could be taken back into RSDL or arrested – speaking out against his confession, or retracting it, was out of the question. And with such tight surveillance, even talking with individual friends online could pose a risk. He was forced to live in the provincial capital of his home province, and not allowed to return to Beijing. Having dinner with friends was for a while out of the question – let alone doing any work as a lawyer.

It would be a long time before he could slowly return to work, and speak more freely, but still without being able to directly challenge the police or retract his confession publically. Wen claims the damage to his reputation continues to limit his ability to work and cooperate with some in the community to this day, but Wen has manage to return to his life's calling, both working representing clients as well as helping other lawyers, training them, offering mentoring.

One direct consequence of the total loss of control suffered in RSDL is his change in habits – from an unhealthy lifestyle, bad food and not taking care of himself, he had instead become health conscious, both for his physical and mental wellbeing.

Chapter 9

Book publisher LAM WING-KEE

PROLOGUE

Lam Wing-kee (林荣基) is the only one of the five notorious Hong Kong booksellers who is truly free and so he is the only one who has been able to tell the truth.

Mr. Lam, now in his early 60s and from Hong Kong, had founded and was managing a small second-floor bookshop in the city called Causeway Bay books that sold gossipy titles about Communist Party members – legal in Hong Kong, banned on the mainland. He was detained in October 2015 as he crossed the border into China. A baseball cap was jammed over his head to cover his eyes, effectively blinded, as officers smuggled him up north on a train to Ningbo, a coastal city on China's east coast. Lam spent the next eight or so months under police's control (in RSDL) there and then later, under heavy surveillance, in a small city in China's south. He was grilled about the banned books and forced to give a confession blaming Swedish citizen Gui Minhai (the publisher) to Beijing-friendly but Hong Kong-based *Phoenix TV*.

Lam's story is based on his own writings, translated into English, expanded slightly through an interview[5].

---

[5] Interview, June 2017.

On the evening of 25 October [2015], cuffed, blindfolded, and wearing a baseball cap, after ten hours on a train. It had only been one day and I had already been taken thousands of miles. As I got off the train, I looked through the side of my blindfolds secretly and caught a glimpse of the bright station sign of Ningbo.

[Later] I was given a document to sign. There were two clauses: one, to promise not to contact my family; two, to promise not to hire a lawyer. Under those circumstances, I was all alone, I could only sign the document. They told me that I was just under "residential surveillance" [at a designated location], but in reality I couldn't even take half a step outside. I couldn't get a lawyer, I couldn't call my family.

The night before [being put on train to Ningbo], I was in Shenzhen tied to a metallic chair, not able to sleep after I was interrogated. [After arriving in Ningbo] my interrogation[s] continued. In November, sessions took place four to five times a week, but at the end of the year they only took place two to three times per week. They brought up questions about co-workers in the bookshop. Names, telephone numbers and addresses of all subscribers, overseas and in mainland China, and even the number of books ordered. Everything was shown clearly. As I viewed the screen, I quietly wondered how they had managed to get the information of readers' book orders. Had they gotten ahold of my key and sent people to the book shop to steal? Could they be so audacious and reckless as to engage in cross-border jurisdiction? Indeed they were audacious and reckless enough to carry out cross-border jurisdiction.

--

The young guards were divided to six groups and took turns guarding me for two hours each in the course of the day. "There is a big guy next door who seems to be your colleague" [one of them said one day]. I had asked him beforehand to help me keep an eye on my surroundings. He nodded lightly and didn't dare say much, because the 300 square foot room was watched by three surveillance cameras.

In the short interval of three months, I felt lonely and helpless. I am not sure if it was the endless interrogations or infinite custody without charge that made me start to consider suicide in just three months. Whenever I looked carefully, I could see that the four walls were covered with soft padding. Obviously, any attempt to break my neck by knocking against the wall would not work. The ceiling was close to 20 feet high, and there was no way I could twist my pants into a rope to hang myself. There was a big inaccessible window, with iron bars blocked by barbed wire which could not pried open with one's bare hands.

"...clearly, long-term solitary confinement and isolation must have resulted in a nervous breakdown for somebody and led to suicide in the past."

The shower head, installed high up, was arc-shaped and nothing could be hung on it. The more one looked at the set-up of the room, the more one got frightened because, clearly, long-term solitary confinement and isolation must have resulted in a nervous breakdown for somebody and led to suicide in the past. All the measures in the room were aimed at preventing suicide. I was probably in such a state of mind when the idea of suicide came up. I think I did not feel too frightened of death itself because, after all, every person must die. It is the fear of death that I feared...

Around the middle of January 2016, they brought a document for me to read. It was a letter of confession regarding a charge against me: "selling books illegally." The letter head read The People's Republic of China. The date - in year, month and day - was given at the bottom. I held my head up. The assistant staff wanted me to sign, similar to the day when I was imprisoned and they asked to sign those statements of giving up my rights. I thought that since I had signed on the previous occasion, there was no way not to sign this time although I knew that such a method was illegal. Fine. Upon signing, Mr. Shi [his chief interrogator] had a more relaxed expression on his face...

Several days later, I was asked to write a letter of remorse. Forcing an innocent person to write a statement of remorse is as equivalently absurd as asking an innocent person to construct his own crime scene. We looked at each other. Perhaps he understood how I felt, and probably wanting to ease things up and get things done he stopped shooting me that ruminating look. Thoughts seemed to rumble through his head as he finally sat down, took a piece of paper, and wrote down five to six main points to guide me through the composition, and told me that this was due tomorrow.

Actually, I had not committed any crime. I did not know how to write such a letter. Somehow, I began like this: "Because I have committed a crime, I now sincerely express regret to the Chinese government ..." With difficulty I waffled on and managed to fill up an A4 sheet. The next day the assistant staff came to take the sheet away, probably to be handed to Mr. Shi for inspection. I thought my half-hearted confession would work. I went to the window and viewed the sky again. The opposite building was visible from this side. Sometimes I gave the excuse of using the toilet and tip-toed on the raised step of the squat toilet to look outside. I counted 20 big windows on the opposite building. It had five storeys, probably the same for the building where I was. There were a few more buildings on the right. If there was no mist, I could see the top of several hills. Later, when they arranged to make video recordings of me, I was moved to another room along the corridor. There, I could see that next to another building at the back was also a small hill. I reckoned that I was detained in a place surrounded by hills on three sides. Misty in the morning and at night, it should be a basin...

Around January to February [2016], I signed the letters of confession and remorse. I thought the case would soon be over...

--

It wasn't the TV station that wanted me to do the TV confession, it was my interrogators. And as far as I know, these TV interviews were broadcast not only on Phoenix TV, but also on CCTV. I made about a dozen [recorded] confessions... It was scripted. There was a director, Mr. Shi.

"[The room] was made up to look like a courtroom; a Mr. Xing acted as the judge, sitting to his side was his assistant playing the part of the deputy judge... I took the prisoner seat."

Throughout there were no journalists, all questions to me were asked by [those] who were interrogating me. I had to answer according to what they wanted [me to say], among them at the last moment one of the guys who had been guarding me was brought in to ask questions too (later I learned that he was a trainee cop, really young, about 20 years old).

TRIAL BY MEDIA
China's new show trials, and the global expansion of Chinese media

The recording process took place six or seven times in the room where I was imprisoned, and three times in another place where they took me there in a seven-seater car. After leaving the building, the drive took about 45 minutes, passing through an express highway and ending up in a big complex with many low-rise houses. All the recording of the so-called confession was conducted in accordance with the script they gave me which I followed. Every time a confession was filmed, there were three or four people present, apart from my two interrogators [one was Mr. Shi]. The questions were first drafted up, and then I had to memorize them... The [material] was all taken from my written confession and statement of repentance. It was Mr Shi who gave me [the black jacket], for the confession recording.

The weirdest incident happened on one occasion when I was taken to a building. After getting out of the car in the carpark, there was a staircase. Probably to save trouble, they removed my eye mask to let me walk the stairs myself. After getting down to the lowest floor and along the passage way, a policewoman walked past by, facing me directly. On her shoulder was the badge of Ningbo Public Security Bureau... [The room] was made up to look like a courtroom; a Mr. Xing acted as the judge, sitting to his side was his assistant playing the part of the deputy judge... I took the prisoner seat. While preparations were being made for the recording, the policewoman came in too, having changed into civilian clothing, and sat by the wall. "Miss Fong?" asked Mr. Shi, who was seated in an interrogator's stand like that in court. The policewoman nodded. He opened the document on the desk and briefly examined it. Then he said it was fine for Miss Fong to remain seated. She nodded. The camera was turned on by the assistant at the back and with the two sitting side by side, questions and answers progressed in sequence, following prior rehearsal. When recording was finished, I asked Mr. Shi out of curiosity, "What was the seated lady doing there?" He removed the recording equipment and answered me at the same time, "She is a witness." I could not withhold my surprise. She was undoubtedly a policewoman, with no connection to my case whatsoever. They found themselves a so-called witness just like that? It was utterly unbelievable how reckless they were, not to mention that the case had been handled in an unlawful manner all along.

--

I could not help worrying because of what happened afterwards. For the purpose of making an application for bail, a remorse video had been made. It was submitted to Beijing along with the letter of remorse. While waiting for news about the outcome, one day I heard Mr. Shi say that the higher authority was not satisfied. What was to be done? I was terribly anxious. If no approval was forthcoming, I would be in jail for the Chinese New Year.

"No one in Hong Kong knows."

Several days later, further news was heard. Beijing would send people here. To observe me, it was said. Right away I felt that it was ominous. One afternoon, two persons came in. I was squatting by the toilet and washing clothes. I hurriedly returned to my seat. I waited till they were seated. I was about to sit down when one of them suddenly banged the table and said I was not allowed to sit. I was startled and had to remain standing. The other person started to talk, "Do you know who we are?" I shook my head, still in shock. Then the other person banged the table also. "We belong to the Central Task Force from Beijing. The kind of books you publish defame our national leaders.

People like you are vicious to the extreme, not worthy of pardon. We can impose proletariat dictatorship over you for ten, twenty years, even till death. No one in Hong Kong knows. We can even pinch you to death like a bug." I was dumbfounded by such a sudden abusive outburst and did not know what to do. I could only stare blankly, incapable of any reaction but to let them continue their rounds of relentless cursing. I had no idea how long the outbursts lasted. I kept standing there. Not until two guards entered later did I realize that they had left. Very clearly, release on bail was out of the question.

Let's make another video; write another letter of remorse, said Mr. Shi later. So the video was remade, and a letter of remorse written again for submission. By then the Chinese New Year was drawing near. Mr. Shi knew I was so worried that I suffered from insomnia. Maybe he wanted to help. He showed a friendly gesture. I am not sure if it was due to similarity in our sentiments or interests, or whether there was some other reason. I understood that he was following orders to interrogate me. He was a little sympathetic towards me, hoping that I could get released on bail. Later, he even said to me that he would be ready to … be my guarantor, as long as I cooperated in the future. At that time I had no choice but to believe him.

--

[One] afternoon, doctors measured my blood pressure. I asked whether Ningbo snowed every year. He shook his head and strapped the wristband around my arm. I said I had never seen snow before, and yet I could not touch it. "It is so beautiful," I said again, "it is way more beautiful than the rain."

Days felt like years to me. As I waited week after week, I received no information that I would be released. One morning, as it was snowing heavily, the doctor came in with a piece of snow. I was overjoyed, feeling the warmth of our shared humanity.

Several months in they let me go to Shaoguan [in south China], where they rented a room for me and intended to keep me long term. There I began my life on bail. I was there from April until June. It was better there. I had a higher degree of freedom. Compared to solitary confinement in Ningbo, where I was not allowed leave my room and could only look up and divine what the signs in the sky meant, Shaoguan was much less confining.

EPILOGUE

In June 2016 Mr. Lam's main interrogator told him he could return to Hong Kong as long as he promised to come back to the mainland with information on a hard disk about his bookshop's mainland customers.

However, after he crossed the border, Mr. Lam held an explosive press conference where he told the story of his capture. He said he had decided to come out and tell the truth for the sake of the "freedom of Hong Kong people." The Chinese government responded with a badly orchestrated smear campaign, and amongst other things, a few weeks' after Mr. Lam's revelations, China's state TV, CCTV, broadcast footage of Mr. Lam in detention and "confessing" in an apparent and unconvincing attempt to discredit him.

During 2018 Lam intended to reopen Causeway Books in the Taiwanese capital of Taipei, as a "symbol of resistance", but last minute several investors pulled out, leaving Lam unable to proceed. In the meanwhile, Chinese encroachment in Hong Kong has continued, including the use of further kidnappings, whilst the Hong Kong government itself realigns more and more with Beijing, most recently by expelling a foreign journalist for critical reporting.

Chapter 10

Forced TV Confessions in China | DINAH GARDNER

The new climate of escalating human rights abuses in China since Xi Jinping took power in 2012 is verging on the unimaginable. The arbitrary detention of as many as one million Uyghur people – a Muslim ethnic group that live in the country's north-western Xinjiang region – into political re-education camps,[1] has horrified the world.

The focus of this book, China's forced TV confessions, and the persecution of the Uyghur both belong to Xi's culture of absolute control and are an updated, high-tech version of the excesses and inhumanities of the Mao era. Starting with the first high-profile televised confession aired in July 2013, over 100 detained individuals have "confessed" on China's state TV and pro-Beijing media, representing 48 cases by August 2018. Despite being a clear violation of Chinese domestic law, universal human rights, a reversal from the country's professed desire to move towards rule of law and an attack on human dignity, the confessions are now well and truly normalized in China.

They transgress basic legal rights such as those to a fair trial and the right to remain silent. As interviews with victims revealed, they are also linked to other abuses such as torture, threats, forced medication, arbitrary detention and solitary confinement.

In particular, they have been used to disproportionally target a section of the population that are seen as enemies or critics of the

TRIAL BY MEDIA
China's new show trials, and the global expansion of Chinese media

party—lawyers, rights activists, journalists and bloggers—who embrace values branded as dangerous western ideas in a secret communication called Document 9 in 2014[2].

Many of the confessions were clearly designed to attract the attention of an overseas audience. That can be seen in the number of non-mainland Chinese victims (14 were foreigners or were Chinese but held overseas passports including from Britain, Sweden, Taiwan, and the US); the fact that several confessions referenced foreign countries or foreign anti-China forces; and the choice of media – the confessions were, without exception, also broadcast on China's overseas state/Party TV channels (CGTN/CCTV9 in English and CCTV4 in Chinese) or by Beijing-friendly mainland and Hong Kong media and posted online. The Chinese Communist Party's (CCP) expanding efforts to export its propaganda and censorship model means this human rights abuse reaches far beyond its borders.[3]

This book, *Trial By Media*, is a continuation of the work of Safeguard Defenders' advocacy report *Scripted and Staged: Behind the scenes of China's forced televised confessions* (2018), which was partly based on research I undertook for a graduate thesis on China's forced televised confessions between 2016 and 2017 at National Chengchi University in Taiwan[4]. It struck me as an important topic to research, not only because it was little studied or understood, but also parading "enemies of the state" on television was something observers associated with rogue regimes, such as North Korea and ISIS, or the struggle sessions of the Mao era. They were shocking because they were reminiscent of the brutality of the old China. What was even more puzzling was this abuse was out in the open—it was being aired on TV around the world for everyone to see. While the domestic audience was familiar with the formula and may have accepted the news segments at face value, foreign audiences were appalled. The global media called them, "Trial by Media."

The first part of my research was recording, watching, transcribing and translating the hours and hours of confession tapes. There were many visual clues that these were "show" confessions beyond the stilted delivery and suspect eye movements of the victims that indicated they were reading from a script—something that was later confirmed with victim interviews. For example, the confessions were always "framed" in one of two ways, which I called "jailhouse" and "neutral." In the first wave of confessions (2013 and 2014), jailhouse was favored. In this, the victim is portrayed as a convicted criminal (despite not being formally charged, undergone trial or usually even having access to a lawyer at that point), dressed in prison clothing (often an orange vest), handcuffed, flanked by police, behind bars and sometimes with their head shaved. From 2015 onwards, for most of the human rights defender victims, neutral settings began to be favored. This was perhaps in response to critical coverage in the western press and an effort to make the confessions look more "legitimate" and less like they were coerced. Here, the victim wears civilian clothes, there are no signs of handcuffs or police, and the background is anonymous— plain wall, office, hotel room and once a restaurant garden.

The wording of the confessions too was suspect and showed obvious signs it was scripted. They were formulaic, containing strikingly similar statements across the years and across the accused "crimes" particularly with human rights defenders. They almost always contained remarks of self-criticism, allegations of colluding with anti-China foreign forces, and unrelated, sometimes inconsequential slurs, on other detainees' behavior, often characterizing them as morally corrupt or professionally negligent. Victims of non-human rights related cases, such as fraud, murder and drugs, talked about the specifics of the alleged crimes, whereas the confessions made in human rights cases were usually much more vague and frequently lacked details of the alleged crime.

I identified three types of statement that stood out because they appeared unusual for a "normal" confession. Called the three D's, they stand for deny, denounce and defend. Defend statements were full of praise for the CCP, its policies, agencies and actions. Denounce statements discredited an "other" – very prevalent in the human rights lawyers group. Deny statements provided the strongest evidence that the Party were using these as a foreign policy tool—they were worded as a direct response to overseas criticism for detaining, sentencing or disappearing a suspect and these either involved foreigners (such as Swedes Peter Dahlin and publisher Gui Minhai) or high-profile victims (rights lawyers Wang Yu and Xie Yang). For example, when overseas NGOs began accusing Beijing of kidnapping Gui from his holiday home in Thailand, he surfaced several months later in a confession video saying bizarrely: "It was my own choice to come back and surrender," and asked the Swedish government not to get involved in his case.

The most startling discoveries came, however, by talking with victims. They were able to reveal the horrific truth behind how these confessions were made. Their experiences were remarkably similar even though their cases were different and separated by several years and across different cities, indicating that "production" of a confession has become systematized in China. Here's what we found out:

Police[6] routinely script and stage the confessions. Suspects are forced to memorize their lines, (or if they can't remember, read them from a screen or cue card). Police order victims on how to deliver their lines; for example, they are told to speak slower or look serious.

---

[6] Here police refers to either state security or regular domestic security.

One victim said he was instructed to cry. Out of shot, police effectively "direct" the confessions. Frequently hours and hours of retakes are made just for a few seconds of airtime. If a victim's "performance" is deemed unacceptable, punishment is sometimes administered. Activist Zhai Yanmin said he was denied food, water and access to a toilet after an "unsatisfactory performance" so that he ended up soiling himself. Victims are often dressed in costume. Day-to-day attire is prison clothing, but they are given civilian clothes to change into for the filming; Hong Kong bookseller Lam Wing-kee's interrogator gave him his winter jacket; Swedish human rights activist Peter Dahlin was told to shower and put on the clothes he was wearing when detained.

The manipulation goes beyond simply staging the confession for the camera. **Police routinely lie about where the confession will be used, denying it will be broadcast on TV and claiming it is for internal use only.** Many only find out once they are released or when they arrive for the confession and they face a CCTV crew. Officers have even tried to explain away the use of CCTV by arguing the state broadcaster is working for the police and the recording will not be aired, as Dr. Liu Sixin experienced. This is likely done to improve the chances that the victim will cooperate. British investigator Peter Humphrey was drugged, chained to a chair and locked inside a cage on the day of his first filmed confession. His interrogators promised that he would only meet print journalists when Mr. Humphrey insisted he did not want to be filmed. CCTV camera lenses poked through the bars of his cage.

Several of the victims said **police used both physical torture as well as forced medication and threats to their family to coerce them into making a taped confession.** Lawyer Wang Yu and activists Mr. Zhai and Liu Xing were told loved ones, such as their children or wife, would suffer or be detained unless they cooperated.

I don't expect everyone to understand. I just want to say that my son is everything to me. Perhaps, I had no other choice. - Wang Yu.

Or as Zhai Yanmin writes, "*They cuffed my hands behind my back, they locked me to iron railings, they would use five or six electric batons to beat me. For a long period they didn't let me eat, or drink water, or go to the bathroom. They subjected me to so many kinds of torture. Yet, it was nothing compared with their threats that they would detain my son.*"

The stories in this book unveil a multitude of other abuses. Mr. Liu was deprived of sleep for days on end and force-fed until his stomach bled when he went on hunger strike to protest his treatment. Mr. Lam became so desperate that he felt suicidal but any plans to end his life were thwarted when he realized his cell was completely padded to be suicide proof; chilling evidence that others before had had similar thoughts.

--

Knowing what we know now – it is both dishonest and unethical for international media to report China's televised confessions at face value. Journalists must use caution when covering future occurrences and include background on their coerced and staged nature. Which is why the *South China Morning Post's* shameful February 2018 coverage of Gui Minhai's third forced television confession was so troubling as well as unprofessional.

It is my wish that this book will help raise awareness about the degrading practice, and will motivate individuals, organizations, media and governments around the world to take forceful action – to condemn and sanction China each time a forced confession is broadcast and for media to report on the practice accurately and ethically. If you have any remaining doubts watch the October 17, 2015 broadcast of Wang Yu and her husband Bao Longjun collapse in tears as they are told on camera about their son's capture and forced to denounce "foreign forces" on television.

The victims of China's televised confessions did not have the opportunity to speak the truth when they were forced in front of the camera to speak the lies of the CCP. This book, finally, offers them the chance to tell the real facts about their ordeal.

Those who spoke to us and still live in China have been immeasurably brave to open up and offer their stories for this book. Psychologically too, it has been no easy endeavor for them, as Ms. Wang explains in her testimony, and with which I will end this chapter.

It is difficult to explain, why I went on television, what kind of mental process I had gone through. And until now, I still feel it is difficult to describe, I don't know how to talk about it. Actually, I do want to talk about it in detail, but I always feel sad. I am still struggling to get over the trauma. But I know I should speak out, even if just in this simple way.

--

DINAH GARDNER | Dinah researched China's forced televised confessions for a graduate program at Taiwan's National Chengchi

University and later for Safeguard Defenders. Prior to that, she worked as a journalist in China for eight years and spent two years studying in Tibet. She is now based in Taipei, Taiwan.

Weaponized media, and responding to China's influencing operations | PETER DAHLIN

Recently there have been two significant developments concerning Chinese media, which were briefly touched upon in the Introduction. They are significant not only because it will change the nature of CCTV and other state media, but will be key in how Chinese influence, and therefore power, expands globally.

One is the rapid expansion in reach, funding, and technical quality of China's state-owned, party-led media, namely CCTV. Since CCTV International's launch of an English-language channel in 2000, it has grown significantly, and will continue to do so as outlined in the 2009-2020 *Master Plan for Chinese media's International Communication*[1], with more than six billion US dollars available. Further plans and investments have followed, including for CCTV to become the only TV station broadcasting in all six United Nations languages. The few times this major expansion has been scrutinized it has largely focused on CCTV and other media's inability to expand its actual reach in terms of viewers, it's still very limited credibility, and it's almost completely absent impact. For now, the investments have been focused on technical developments and new facilities, rather than increasing quality in content.

At the same time, and parallel to this, these has been significant successes in regards to another development. It concerns an issue that has gone largely unnoticed, outside of New Zeeland and Australia, about how the Chinese Communist Party has scored major successes in taking control over foreign-based independent Chinese-language media. In Australia this takeover is now largely complete, with almost all independent Chinese language media outlets, most often local newspapers and radio stations, now under effective CCP control[2]. The same process, as exposed in Emily Feng's reporting in Financial Times, is ongoing in North America and Europe[3], with little to no scrutiny paid.

As English and other language channels of the CCP's official media is rapidly expanding, and alongside a takeover of independent Chinese-language media, Chinese media companies have also gone on a buying spree, especially in Africa, buying stakes in existing local media, with the expected result of muting voices critical of China, and, just as importantly, muting these media's role in investigating their own governments in their home countries.

It's hard to not look at these different but related trends and not imagine that it's all a coordinated effort. With the 13th National Congress in March 2018[4], with the world focused on the abolishing of term limits for Xi Jinping, the coordinated effort behind all this became clear to those who paid attention. It itself wasn't a new process, but with a massive reorganization of several bodies dealing with media and propaganda, the purpose and form behind these different trends became clearer.

Reorganization of Chinese media

"Winning hearts and minds at home and abroad through United Front work is crucial to realizing the great rejuvenation of the Chinese people"[5]

TRIAL BY MEDIA
China's new show trials, and the global expansion of Chinese media

During the March Congress several major changes were announced. These changes concern both the state and party organs who directs and manages the media organizations, as well as that of the media organizations as well.

One such change was that the media in charge of China's expanded overseas ambitions would be brought more tightly under party rather than state control. With this, it's more correct to refer to CCTV and Xinhua as party rather than state media.

This echoed Xi's earlier call for all media to obey not the state but the Chinese Communist Party, and to pledge absolute loyalty to the party,[6] which following the Congress is now essentially synonymous with Xi Jinping himself. For greater effectiveness, something that has eluded Chinese party-media's overseas' work for so long, CCTV, along with China Radio International and Chinese National Radio, is to be merged into the *Central Radio and Television Network*, which for its international operations will be named *Voice of China*. With that, China will create what will likely be the largest media brand in the world, with around the clock TV stations broadcasting in all six UN languages, and radio broadcasts in over 60 languages spanning 170 countries or regions around the globe. In size and reach, this represents the creation of a global propaganda machine the likes of which the world has never seen.

Along with more superficial changes, such as changing the name, comes far more important changes, such as about the control of the media. Earlier, control of China's media resided partly with the state organ SARFT - State Administration of Radio, Film, and Television (name later changed to SAPPFRT - State Administration of Press, Publication, Film, Radio, and Television) and partly with the party's Propaganda Department (Central Propaganda Department), and its sub-bureau for 'External News'. With the restructuring program, the state organ's role was transferred to the Propaganda department, which assumed full and total control[7]. The same body would with this reorganization also take full control over the film and TV industry in China[8], continuing a process of "unifying party leadership" over more and more cultural, media and news output.

The institutional restructuring plan was announced by the Xinhua news agency shortly after the Congress, the *Program for the Deepening Reform of Party and Government Organs*[9]. The sections outlined in the program are not, in many ways, new to observers of Chinese media, but taken together they show the direction of China's media re-organization.

The creation of the National Radio and Television Administration seeks to *"centralize and unify CCP leadership of news and public opinion work"* and to *"develop the role of radio and television into the mouthpiece of the party",* and take over the responsibilities of an earlier state organ. The same section in the program specifies that the chief responsibility of this new organ, which directs the work of CCTV and the soon to be named media behemoth Voice of China, is to *"implement the Party's propaganda guidelines and policies",* *"to supervise, manage and censor the content and quality of radio, television and online audiovisual programming"* and, importantly for its international expansion, *"to coordinate the promotion of the going out [overseas] of the radio and television section."*[10]

As for the creation of the new media behemoth itself, the program makes the purpose behind the reorganization clear:

Adherence to correct guidance of public opinion, placing a high priority on the building and innovation of dissemination methods, raising the dissemination force, guiding force, influence and credibility of news and public opinion.[11]

If the above shows the purpose of the reorganization, the below, also from the program, presents what the new media giant is tasked with:

Its principal responsibilities will be to propagate the theories, political line and policies of the Party; to plan and manage major propaganda reports; to organize the production of radio and television; to produce and broadcast premium radio and television products; to channel hot social topics; to strengthen and improve supervision by public opinion, to promote the integrated development of multimedia; to strengthen the building of international broadcasting capacity; to tell China's story well.[12]

The strengthening role of the CCP in China's media and its international operations is one of several aspects of this reorganization. At the same time, the United Front Work Department (UFWD), a party organ, underwent a major reorganization as well. First off, it absorbed the *Overseas Chinese Affairs Office*[13], which has been responsible for liaison with the overseas Chinese community. To understand the importance of this body, it should be noted this is the body that has run *China News Service* (CNS), a news agency aimed the overseas Chinese diaspora, and which has played a key role in China's takeover of independent Chinese language media internationally, described in detail further below.

The UFWD is a little-known entity (outside of China), but one that plays a very important role. It is with the UFWD that the general responsibility for controlling the Chinese diaspora lies, and relates not only to media control but running Confucius institutes'[7], liaison with student groups, cultural associations, etc., and is related to any work seeking to co-opt Chinese communities outside of mainland China.

As Peter Mattis, a security analyst in the U.S. stated in his testimony to the *U.S.-China Economic and Security Review Commission*: "The CCP continues to lay the groundwork in the United States for United Front operations that could be similar to those that have achieved success in some U.S.-allied countries" (referring to Australia and New Zeeland).[14] The fact that Xi Jinping has created a small leading group[8] on UFWD, with himself as its head, should make it abundantly clear just how important this body is, and how much importance XI Jinping places on its duties.

Any discussion on Chinese influencing operations abroad leads back to the UFWD, a body referred to by Xi Jinping in a speech as one of the CCP's "magic weapons"[15]. Or as Australian researcher in Chinese studies Gerald Groot puts it: "United Front Work is now of direct relevance and sometimes concern to an increasing number of foreign governments, notably Australia, Zealand, Canada and the United States. United Front Work abroad is not limited to only these countries though."[16] The head of the UFWD made it clear: "we need to fully and better understand the use of this 'magic weapon'."[17]

---

[7] Confucius institutes are educational non-profit institutes funded by the Chinese state outside of China, offering language classes, and hosting events to promote Chinese culture. The institutes are often located on campuses. The institutes are set up at educational institutions in foreign countries, and the Chinese government will share the cost.
[8] Ad hoc supra-ministerial coordinating and consulting body, formed to take the lead on issues that cut across the government, party, and military systems.

The UFWD cultivates academic and cultural exchanges with the world outside China, advises on mergers and acquisitions that could be useful for the purpose of the UFWD, and even to seek to appoint foreigners to positions in Chinese companies or Chinese-funded entities in host countries[18], all of which ultimately, just like CCTV, seeks to expand Chinese influence in the target countries.

The changes we will soon see on CCTV, changing its name and logo, are thus, as can be seen from above, a very minor part of a much larger change underneath, changes made for two specific purposes, one, to expand the influence, and thus power, of China, and two, to put more of that power in the hands of the CCP, and, ultimately, Xi Jinping himself.

The (temporary) setbacks of state media's international expansion

On September 30, 2018 a CCTV journalist based in the United Kingdom, Kong Linlin, attended an event by the Human Rights Committee of the UK's Conservative Party, focused on the deteriorating freedoms in Hong Kong, and increased violations by China of the "one country, two systems" framework. While Benedict Rogers, a well-known human rights activist and co-chair of the committee spoke, Kong Linlin started loudly shouting, accusing some attendees as traitors, and calling for the activists there to stop interfering in China's internal affairs. The whole spectacle was rather embarrassing.

With this development, which caught the International media's imagination, and which was also widely discussed on Chinese social media, came a number of articles from well-known China hands like Jeremy Goldkorn[19], former state media worker James Palmer[20] and comments from journalists like Rose Luqiu[21]. Their comments largely ran along the same idea, that her (Kong Linlin's) behavior largely signified a key reason why China's state media has had such an abysmal record in success, namely that her actions were aimed not so much to improve the work of CCTV in the UK, obviously, but to please her bosses in Beijing, who might consider such political outbursts a sign of loyalty.

This idea is not new. A number of academic articles were released in volume 13 (issue 1) of the Westminster Papers in Communication and Culture[22], focused largely on CCTV's expansion and operations in South America. A common thread, along with CCTV's dismal performance in increasing viewership and their continued lack of credibility, even when compared with Russia Today (RT) and Iran's HipanTV, was the inability of local bureaus to adapt to the target countries, and how all editorial control continues to be in the hand of Beijing.

One study showed that CGTN-Español, the Spanish language channel, has limited reach, with many simply unaware of its existence. When knowledge about it did exist, most knew that it was a state-backed channel and gave it very low credibility.[23]

In comparison to other state-backed media in the region, CCTV was perceived as more strongly controlled by a foreign government. The production of content, often in a traditional newscast setting, follows the form of presentation inside China – a style that many in the west will think of as *very* rigid and authoritarian - and one that highlights the challenges of localization. This failure to adapt is unlikely to be because they are unaware that its mode of presentation is ineffectual, but because the local bureaus primarily answer to their bosses in Beijing. Like with Kong Linlin, local bureaus primarily seek the approval of those in Beijing, the same people who handle domestic media in China where the mode of delivery is 'conservative' at best.

TRIAL BY MEDIA
China's new show trials, and the global expansion of Chinese media

Simply put, the stilted 'propaganda mode' of content delivery may work in China, but stands little chance of success internationally. However, the political structure and governance model makes it impossible for local bureaus to adapt, a consequence of the highly politicized system it operates within. Pleasing Beijing is a requirement for keeping one's career.

Another study, covering 2014, showed that the four bureaus in South America – in Argentina, Cuba, Mexico, and Venezuela - employing close to 100 people, consisted of 75% Chinese nationals[9]. No non-Chinese held any key position.[24]

Similar studies have shown that investment so far has been into new facilities and improved technical capabilities, and not learning how to adapt media broadcasts to local standards and forms that may actually work.[25]

Similar failure in gaining credibility is visible in Africa, although analyzed not by looking at viewers of CCTV, but the perception of CCTV and other Chinese media by local leaders around Africa.[26]

For anyone worried about unchecked development of Chinese media abroad, there is some comfort in seeing that despite announced plans and investment packages, CCTV has had little to no success in its expansion, if measured in impact. It remains unknown to most potential viewers, and in the case of it being known, is seen as a propaganda outlet. However, with time, despite continued focus on 'political purity' as judged by the bosses in Beijing, and with continued inability to localize its content and delivery, CCTV is set to expand its influence. The sheer amount of money, billions of dollars, will at some point start having an effect. Likewise, this development is but one of several ones, working in tandem, and need be taken seriously, as it will

---

[9] Included in these figures is also the small Spain bureau, grouped together due to shared language.

have an impact on the future information dissemination system in their target countries.

Despite CCTVs abject failure, China has managed to improve its image abroad, and even though no surveys exist, anecdotal evidence suggests that it has also managed to co-opt large sections of the Chinese diaspora internationally into the arms of the CCP. This is a direct objective of the UFWD, the umbrella organization in which CCTV and other media is just one of several players, and in this regard, the United Work Front's work has been a striking success. How? Because of the takeover of formerly independent Chinese language media abroad, through Chinese party media, and the UFWD own China News Service (CNS).

"Borrowing boats to go to sea" – co-opting foreign Chinese language media

"Borrowing boats to go to sea", meaning to use another's resources to fulfil one's goals.

The United Front Work Department, tasked with co-opting the Chinese diaspora outside of Mainland China, works through many instruments. The most well-known of these are likely the Confucius Institutes that have spread across the world, offering language and "culture" training, in line with the CCP's political agenda. However, many consulates and embassies have also been given an outsized role in co-opting these communities. Some of this relate to student groups and associations of Chinese students at Universities abroad[27], and as Professor Feng Chongyi in Australia says "they control almost all the community associations".[28] In fact, reading the handbook for UFWD is like reading an instruction book for espionage and source cultivation[29].

It is within the framework of the UFWD and the expansion of China's state or party media that the takeover of independent Chinese language media across the globe should be analyzed.

Thanks to the extensive data collection and reporting by Financial Times' Emily Feng, the picture on how this process has unfolded and developed has become clearer. Essentially, small local newsrooms, often newspapers, printing in Chinese language and for an exclusively Chinese readership, is offered various forms of partnerships with state media organizations in China. These partnerships provide the local media with select content for them to publish, free of charge, often under their own masthead with little to no indication that the material is produced by China's party or state media. Some partnerships also mean said local papers must also run inserts from their partner, often the People's Daily or China News Service.

The partnerships places the local media in a position of economic dependency of the CCP.

Through hundreds of such news partnerships, China is moving to silence any dissenting Chinese language media, and allow all Chinese language media, at home and abroad, to speak with one voice, the voice of the CCP. In New Zeeland and Australia, the initial primary targets, the process has neared completion.

The effectiveness of this campaign is the dual approach of offering content to cash-starved local newsrooms, along with penalties for those not willing to toe the line. "The CCP is trying to 'merge' or 'fuse', in their own words, overseas Chinese media content with its own or with some of the people that are in key roles with domestic media in China," says Anne-Marie Brady, a China expert at the University of

Canterbury in New Zealand. "This is a really well established phenomenon. It is just that the outside world hasn't noticed."[30]

As part of the UFWD, Chinese embassies and consulates take an active role in their respective communities. Professor Feng says he sees these consulates working to notify potential advertisers about not advertising in local newspapers who have chosen to not toe the CCP-line. Others repeat the same line, seeing how local papers critical, or even neutral, to Beijing, sees it losing its ad revenue. Some of this, perhaps even most of it, may be a consequence of self-censorship. Many local businesses who may advertise in their local papers depend on business relationships with China to a much greater extent than before, and will be wary of supporting any news outlet deemed critical of Beijing. The end result is the same, starving of already cash-strapped newsroom, forcing them to either accept a more pro-Beijing line and partnerships with Chinese media, or see themselves ruined and replaced by competitors.

The consequences of this process should not be underestimated. In Australia, an editor at a pro-Beijing publication told the Sydney Morning Herald: "Nearly 95 percent of the Australian Chinese newspapers have been brought in by the Chinese government to some degree."[31] Even if this figure is hyperbole, the fact that a pro-Beijing editor would use such strong language makes it clear the process, even if not yet entirely complete, has been a striking success. An editor in Australia, speaking on condition of anonymity, said: "Advertisers, usually Chinese-owned firms or businesses which rely on good relations with the Chinese government, are told by consulate officials to pull advertising from non-compliant media outlets, and are directed instead to divert their dollars to those who toe the party line."[32]

TRIAL BY MEDIA
China's new show trials, and the global expansion of Chinese media

Individual writers and staff reporters who don't toe the line in their writing can see themselves fired quickly. [33] Others are less fortunate. Chen Xiaoping, editor of New York-based Mirror Media Group who has published news contrary to Beijing's wishes, had his Chinese wife detained and disappeared in China. Later she was made to give what is very close to a Forced TV Confession, in a video uploaded online. Chen has not been able to reach his wife since she was detained.

Along the takeover of Chinese media in Australia, China has made all of Australia's key English language media, except public broadcaster ABC, sign partnership deals with Chinese state media, including respected newspapers such as Sydney Morning Herald/The Age. In China this deal was much touted as a major victory, in Australia on the other hand, it was meet with silence[34].

Anne-Marie Brady is a China expert at the University of Canterbury in New Zealand who specializes in Chinese media operations in New Zeeland. After she spoke publicly on the issue both her home and office were burglarized.

Another issue has been the investment spree into foreign media, another trend that seeks the same result. Azad Essa in South Africa, a long-time weekly columnist realized this when, as one of his many columns, he published a piece on the situation in Xinjiang about the mass incarceration and disappearances of Uyghurs. It took only a few hours before he was told the column was not to be printed. A day later his entire column was canceled. It shouldn't have surprised him[35]. His paper is owned by Independent Media, the second largest media group in South Africa, and is now part-owned by a Chinese firm with links to the Chinese state (China International Television Corporation (CITVC) and the China-Africa Development Fund (CADFUND))[36].

As Azad notices, alongside investing in its own media in Africa, as part of the "going out" policy, there has also been a major increase in investment in existing local African media. It's not for nothing that CCTV's second division after the Americas was not European, which at time of writing is only just now being set up, but African, headquartered in Nairobi, Kenya. It goes along with an African edition of China Daily, and a monthly magazine (ChinAfrica), both based in South Africa. It is however with investment in private media where success has been seen, not through mouthpieces like CCTV and China Daily.

If media partnerships as a means of taking over independent Chinese media at first focused on Australia and New Zeeland, and investment into private media have so far focused on Africa, both trends are coming to the fore in both North America and Europe.

Financial Times' expose identified over 200 such partnerships. "This is not even being done in the dark or hidden". As Emily Feng says when conducting the research, "it's all out there, freely available, it's just that no one seems to pay attention"[37].

Through the research, 44 such partnerships with European media has been observed[38], most of them with either People's Daily, a party-owned newspaper, or China New Service, an organ controlled by the UFWD. As with the rest of the world, most partnerships are with newspapers, but some also target TV and radio. More shockingly, the amount of these partnerships has exploded, with some 204 partnerships (new ones, as well as renewal of old ones) found in 2016-2017, compared to between 26 and 57 for the three periods preceding it (2010/11, 2012/13, 2014/15). The picture for North America looks similar. As a tactic, it's both expanding rapidly, and working very well to silence all dissent and co-opt the Chinese diaspora.

Outside of writers being fired, an editor having his wife disappeared, and foreign academics targeted, like Anne-Marie Brady, there are also more broad consequences. An editor from Australia made it clear: "The end result is that almost all the Australian Chinese newspapers only publish what the Chinese government wants them to".[39]

The loss of independence of Chinese language media abroad, now more and more repeating and reinforcing China's party and state media, combined with a push for partnerships between party or state media and desperate but well respected foreign media, such as the Washington Post to Sydney Morning Herald, along with the massive expansion of China's own English and other language media, will undoubtedly have consequences. The only thing that has limited the impact so far has been some resistance from some media in the west to enter such relationships, and CCTV's own complete failure to adapt to local environments in its content and delivery style.

Put it more bluntly, the combination of greater economic dependency on China, along with political influencing operations and expanded media control will have direct consequences.

The threat of China's influencing operations

As J. Michael Cole writes in a recently released report on China's attempt at developing expanded influence and power, these influencing operations *"...are meant to undermine state and democratic institutions and thereby facilitate Beijing's objectives in those societies. Unsurprisingly, influence operations have also sought to exploit what revisionist regimes like the CCP regard as a strategic opportunity to alter the liberal-democratic order that has governed international relations since the end of the Second World War. In particular, China's leaders see opportunity amid signs of a democratic backsliding characterized by the Trump election in the US, the advent of Brexit, and crypto-fascism in Europe."[40]*

As Chinese media is the media of the Chinese Communist Party, and because the CCP view its expansion as a weapon in a greater soft power struggle, it's easy to understand why Chinese media's expansion abroad is a threat. The amount of money spent, and the focus, from the highest level, in developing China's media internationally should speak volumes in and of itself. However, its media is but one part of a far greater push, and which taken together represents a far greater threat.

First off, Chinese media operations will become more effective, with time, as its need for a greater voice dictates improvements must be made. It will become clearer to party central after the current reorganization and investment round are completed, and once it's noted that they despite this still have little to no impact.

It is also safe to say that the media organizations' will be forced to act more upon market logic than before. This alone will force their media operations to localize, and therefore become more impactful. The Chinese "economic miracle" is over, and China will at best enter a new phase of "mid-level" growth, and simply won't be able to afford to have all its media operate on such a massive scale without at least some consideration to reach, and impact. With the scope of investment, such an increase in efficiency could have significant effect on the CCPs ability to control debates and information flows.

However, CCTV (and other media) does not operate alone. It is one important weapon along political influencing campaigns directed both by the United Front Work Department, the Ministry of Commerce and the State Council, alongside taking control over independent foreign-based Chinese language media, cultivating economic-cultural-political ties, and through strategic investments in the media sector. All this exist together, with a similar goal, a goal clearly spelled out in the work duties of the UFWD, and actually in the duties of CCTV and its controlling organ. None of this is really hidden, it's just not discussed, except perhaps in the first key target countries – Australia and New Zeeland.

Australia and New Zeeland, key allies of the U.S. and the loosely defined "western alliance" are good examples.

Not long ago, New Zealand's then Minister of Defense, Jonathan Coleman, admitted that New Zealand was currently "walking this path between the US and China [41]. This followed signing a *Comprehensive Strategic Partnership Agreement* with China in 2014, and expanding ties not only in agriculture, finance, and tourism but also in telecommunications, education, and even defense. [42] In a briefing to the new Prime Minister of New Zeeland in December 2017, it was said that "activities in New Zealand over the past year have included attempts to access sensitive government and private sector information, and attempts to unduly influence expatriate communities" [43], echoing the work of the UFWD. David Shambaugh, director of the China policy programme at George Washington University said it well when he said that: "The party under Xi [Jinping] believes it is engaged in a 'discourse war' — with the west, which it thinks enjoys media hegemony and must be challenged".[44]

In recent months, Australia has said it is concerned about Chinese intelligence operations and covert campaigns influencing the country's politics.[45] They should be, because now, including in the upper echelons of politics, there is an actual ongoing discussion about whether Australia should move away from the U.S. towards China, including in areas of politics and security. For New Zeeland, the country is considered so compromised by Chinese influence that during a review of the *U.S.-China Economic and Security Review Commission* has called into question its continued membership in the "five eyes" intelligence cooperation: "...need to have a discussion about whether or not New Zealand can remain, given this problem with the political core." [46]

Azad Essa, writing on Chinese investment in African media[47], sees a bigger picture, and how its unfolding will hurt African countries themselves. "Companies that take on Chinese ownership are likely to experience the Chinese model of censorship; red lines are thick and non-negotiable. Given the economic dependence on the Chinese and crisis in newsrooms, this is rarely confronted. And this is precisely the type of media environment that China wants their African allies to replicate." With this in mind, it's not surprising to learn that Faith Muthambi, then (South African) minister for communications, went to China "to understand how the country's state-owned broadcast media works"[48]. What real reason other than to learn how to control news, control information, could such a trip possibly be for? And this, of course, makes perfect sense, for China to reach out to control the media there, they are just as likely to want to control the message it sends about its local partners. Censoring about China will likely extend to censoring about the host country itself, limiting investigative and critical reporting in those countries.

In Canada, back in 2010, at a time when Chinese operations were far more modest than now, the director of Canada's national intelligence agency warned that several Canadian provincial cabinet ministers and government employees were "agents of influence" for foreign countries, particularly China.

Germany's office for the Protection of the Constitution recently accused Beijing using social media to target lawmakers and other government employees. According to a New York Times report, Chinese agents posed as leaders of think tanks and headhunters, and offered all-expenses-paid trips to China and meetings with influential clients.[49] Similar offers of all expenses paid trips are used to invite foreign Chinese language media editors, often organized under blandly named forums and meetings, to push for media partnerships. CNS, CCTV, and the People's Daily also organize such forms regularly.

The U.S. itself, as can be seen in the hearings with the *U.S.-China Economic and Security Review Commission*, has looked at the UFWD and Chinese media in Australia as a means of preparing itself for what it considers the inevitable; a concerted effort directed at the U.S. Even though such a strategy is likely already being put in place, Europe and the EU is likely to be a target of equal stature, seeing that China's economy depends on the EU more than any other trade partner. The battle is coming to Europe, a continent that, unlike North America, seems woefully unprepared, with neither knowledge, interest nor will to deal with it.

Addressing CCTV's abuses on Forced TV Confessions

Coinciding with the final touches on this book, British victim of two forced TV confessions, Peter Humphrey, together with Safeguard Defenders, filed a *Fairness and Privacy Complaint* with Ofcom – the United Kingdom's Office of Communications. Based on Ofcom's *Broadcasting Code*, which they are legally mandated to enforce for all broadcast license holders in the UK, and the precedent on its handling of another nation's (Iran's) media proven to have used a forced TV confession, it will be of utmost difficulty to deny the complaint and not launch an investigation, and any such investigation, unless there is undue political influence, will see CCTV convicted. It is, from the perspective of the underlying law Ofcom is set to enforce, an open and shut case. A case identical to this one that saw Iran's *Press TV* have its license to broadcast in the UK revoked. Except, in the case of CCTV, the same behavior can be proven to be systematic.

This, the use of existing regulatory bodies, is by far the most potent, and perhaps the only, tool available, in not just one but in many countries, in how the outside world can address China's use of forced TV confessions, and powerful tool that stands a good chance of succeeding, if employed.

The UK's Ofcom has been used as a start because it stands as a giant among TV broadcast regulatory bodies, with a wide scope to act, and because in the UK all those who broadcast to the UK, not just those broadcasting *from* or *in* the UK, must have a license. This is unlike Sweden, for example, whose regulatory body – *Granskningsnämnden* – is weak to the point of being useless.

With what's at stake with CCTV and other media's expansion in Europe, and how high a value it seems the CCP places on it, logic would dictate that an investigation by Ofcom, and an appropriate penalty for CCTV, will force the CCP to reconsider whether CCTV should broadcast these forced TV confessions. For foreign victims in China, that likely means CCTV will also cease to partake in extracting, recording, producing such confessions, thus directly affecting their role in denying these victims their right to a fair trial. It will likely have less of an impact on the victims who are Chinese nationals, but some of those "confessions" also have a clear foreign audience, so the impact would not be insignificant either.

Looking at the increase in co-opting local Chinese media around Europe, and the increasing alarm in both media and with governments around Europe at increased attempts at both espionage and more general political influencing, China is now taking activities earlier limited to Australia and New Zealand, to Europe. Europe is becoming a new target of a concerted influencing operation. The reason is easy to understand – Europe and the EU is a vast trading partner, and is becoming even more important as trade friction with the United States mounts. With slowing growth in China, that importance is set to further increase.

The opening of a new production center in London, as the basis for a future European division, also shows the importance of Europe to CCTV and the expansion of its media. The UK center is set to have 350 journalists, more than double that of either its Washington, DC or Nairobi equivalent[50]. China is serious about establishing its official voice in Europe.

With this in mind, no matter how important they may feel about being able to broadcast forced TV confessions in Europe, or other international markets, will it come close to the importance of the opening and running of its European division? Of course not.

Ofcom should rightfully revoke CCTV's license, and based on precedent, will be hard to avoid doing. If so, CCTV will without a doubt be instructed to cease airing these confessions while a new license is applied for. But even a lesser penalty, from placing them under probation and heightened scrutiny, to a monetary fine, would likely have the same effect. The CCP will not risk losing their media empire's international arm just to broadcast forced TV confessions.

Proper action by Ofcom will likely also encourage media regulators in other core international markets to consider similar action, and by no means will the action of Ofcom only have an effect on broadcasts in Europe, but likely all international broadcasts. A greater focus of CCTV collaboration in committing gross human rights violations inside China, including for domestic victims whose confession broadcasts are only for a domestic audience, is likely to benefit, although those violations are unlikely to cease entirely, unless Magnitsky Act type sanctions are imposed.

Addressing China's influencing operations

The Magnitsky Act is a tool built for countering gross human rights violations being carried out by state agents. It is also a tool that continues to spread, most recently becoming a very real possibility on EU level in Europe, where several countries themselves have already adopted it. It is not a tool to counter political influencing operations per se, but a tool to counter any person or bodies shown to have committed gross human rights violations and therefore those persons or bodies' ability to operate internationally.

We owe a great deal of gratitude to investment banker William Browder of Hermitage Capital for the existence of this new tool. His lawyer, Sergei Magnitsky, was by most accounts tortured to death in detention in Russia for having exposed extensive corruption. William Browder's tireless campaigning led to the United States adopting the first Magnitsky Act, aimed at Russia. With this act, the U.S. can sanction individuals proven to have committed gross human rights violations. Its reach was later expanded with the Global Magnitsky Act. Sanctions available varies from different countries' acts, but range from travel bans to assets freezing and beyond. As it targets individuals, and those individuals' ill-gotten gains from such violations, it is potentially very powerful. Canada, the UK, and all three Baltic States have followed suit and established such acts.

Only with the mass atrocities being carried out in Xinjiang, where as many as one million Muslim minority people – Uyghurs mostly – have been placed into camps, without any due process, in a system that is beginning to rival the Soviet Union's Gulag system in scale, have there been calls to apply the Magnitsky Act to perpetrators in China on larger scale. However, even before it has been applied to individuals. Chinese media personnel, oftentimes, need access to international travel, and also the use of banking and ownership of assets. Those proven to partake in human rights violations should be a natural target for the Magnitsky Act, both because they deserve it, and because as targets they can be effective to stop, or limit, the behavior.

CCTV journalist Dong Qian, who has been known to have been the journalist who partook in making several (at least five) of the forced TV confession we have data on[10], is one such ripe target, a symbolic target that would send shockwaves within Chinese state media.

There have also been growing calls, although ones meet with tough resistance, in the EU, to establish a body to analyze, supervise and perhaps even have a regulatory say in, key investments in the EU, an issue that was raised further by an audit conducted by Bloomberg[51]. Its review found that many, perhaps more than half, of all investments made by China (their state-controlled companies) in the EU would not be possible in reverse, i.e., EU companies cannot make the same investments in China. As such investment is likely to spread towards media, and thus media control, such a body, not itself aimed at China, could play a key role in guarding both against unfair trade practices with China, but to protect its media from undue political controlling by the CCP.

Limiting Chinese influencing operations can also be managed by properly responding to Chinese actions. Despite China's ever-mounting and clear violations of international law, going so far as to kidnap EU citizens outside of China, and despite more forceful

---

[10] Including Wang Yu, Liu Sixin, Zhai Yanmin, Liu Xing and the failed attempt to record one with Wu Gan.

intervention into domestic politics, as has been seen in Sweden during 2018, at no point has China faced threat of expulsion of diplomats or spies, the same ones responsible for controlling the Chinese diaspora in Europe, and in effect, responsible for turning that diaspora against their adopted home countries. Likewise, Xinhua news agency, a well-known front both for hosting (giving cover) spies from the Ministry of State Security, and for having their reporters conduct espionage themselves, could easily, if placed under scrutiny, be punished for such unlawful acts.

Recent news reporting on significant refugee and immigrant espionage in Sweden, both on the Tibetan and Uyghur populations, have made it clear how active the MSS and their diplomatic missions are, even in a country like Sweden with very small Tibetan and Uyghur populations.

In all these cases, it's not a matter of tools not existing, but rather that those tools are not applied to China.

There are also other considerations, which firmly aligns with the discussions being heard more and more related to China's unfair trade practices. Gao Bingchen, a Canadian-Chinese columnist, says "The biggest problem is the lack of reciprocity. Western society helps Chinese culture and content by freely disseminating it, but China is completely closed off to content from western countries"[52]

If China's expansion of its media is part for its political influencing specifically, it's also part of a larger soft power struggle. Gao gets its completely right when he posits the unfair balance in this relationship. Even from an economic perspective it makes little sense that China is allowed to sell its "product" in, for example, the U.S., while the U.S. equivalent cannot sell theirs in China. Solely based on fair trade practices, why is Chinese media given free access across the globe, but no foreign media has access (to broadcast or print) to China? We often hear about some individual correspondent for a foreign media, only there to gather information for media broadcasts outside China, having their visa revoked, but rarely do we talk about the much larger problem, namely lack of equal access.

The same problem applies to many, even most, and certainly an increasing amount of, sectors of the Chinese economy. Either those sectors are entirely blocked off from the world economy, or foreign competition can only operate under severe restrictions. These days Chinese officials do not even hide it anymore, often saying a variation of "the price for foreign companies to operate in China (when possible at all), is for them to give us their technology".

The answer to the rise of China and the international expansion of CCP propaganda should never be to censor it, or to limit that conversation. But no conversation can be had in the current mode. It's one hand trying to clap. Anyone who believes in a free exchange of ideas, of free media, must first realize that it's based on competition, a competition of ideas. For that to be possible, China's access must be based on the access they give. We should welcome CCTV in Europe, for example, but such must be based on China welcoming European media in China. The only way to achieve this is to apply Tit for Tat, the same objective the current trade struggle claim to try to achieve. You can sell your cars here when we can sell our cars there. Tit for Tat.

For an exchange of idea, China must be forced to operate under the same rules we do, or face Tit for Tat sanctions. Or as noted in a paper released recently by the respected Mercator Institute for China Studies:

"China takes advantage of the one-sided openness of our democratic societies. The three principal targets of Chinese sharp power are political and economic elites; media and public opinion; and civil society, grassroots, and academia."[53] This should serve as a suitable

ending to this book, and to reiterate the need for closer scrutiny of China's significant expansion plans for its media and its influence.

TRIAL BY MEDIA
China's new show trials, and the global expansion of Chinese media

Database of forced TV confession events |
APPENDIX

For full database, continuously updated, with many more variables for each confession, see **https://rsdlmonitor.com/forced-tv-confessions-database/**.

#	Date of broadcast	Main confessor (or target)	Nationality	Legal status when FC
1	2013-07-15	Liang Hong (main)	CN	
		Weng Jianyong (supporting)	CN	Detention
2	2013-08-22	Qin Huohuo (main)	CN	Arrest
		Lier Chaisi (main)	CN	Arrest
3	2013-08-27	Peter Humphrey (main)	U.K.	Arrest
4	2013-08-29	Charles Xue Biqun (main)	U.S.	Detention
		Ms Zhang (supporting)	CN	Detention
		Ms Liang (supporting)	CN	Detention
		Ms Ma (supporting)	CN	Detention
		Ms Wang (supporting)	CN	Detention
		Ms Li (supporting)	CN	Detention
5	2013-09-15	Charles Xue Biqun (main)	U.S.	Detention
6	2013-09-29	Dong Liangjie (main)	CN	Detention
		Charles Xue Biqun (supporting)	U.S.	Detention

TRIAL BY MEDIA
China's new show trials, and the global expansion of Chinese media

7	2013-10-17	Dong Rubin (main)	CN	Arrest
		Hou Peng (supporting)	CN	Arrest
		Mr Du (supporting)	CN	Free
		Mr Wang (supporting)	CN	Free
8	2013-10-22	Ge Qiwei (main)	CN	
9	2013-10-26	Chen Yongzhou (main)	CN	Detention or Arrest
10	2014-01-26	Li Gang (main)	CN	Arrest
11	2014-05-08	Gao Yu (main)	CN	Detention
12	2014-05-13	Xiang Nanfu (main)	CN	Detention
13	2014-05-31	Zhang Lidong (main)	CN	Arrest
14	2014-06-25	Mirzat (main)	CN (UI)	
15	2014-06-26	Ning Caishen (main)	CN	Administrative detention
16	2014-06-29	Zhang Yuan (main)	CN	Administrative detention
17	2014-07-14	Peter Humphrey (main)	U.K.	Arrest
		Yu Yingzeng (supporting)	CN	Arrest
18	2014-08-04	Guo Meimei (main)	CN	Detention
		3 others (blurred) (supporting)	CN	

19	2014-08-19	Ko-Chen-tung (main)	TW	Administrative detention
20	2014-08-27	Nurmemet Abidilimit (main)	CN (UI)	Detention or Arrest
		Ghesi Hasan (supporting)	CN (UI)	
21	2014-09-25	Wang Xin	CN	Arrested
22	2014-09-26	Ilham Tohti (main) (offscreen target)	CN (UI)	Prison
		Luo Yuwei (supporting)	CN (Yi)	Arrest
		Perhat Halmurat (supporting)	CN (UI)	Arrest
		Shohret Nijat (supporting)	CN (UI)	Arrest
23	2014-09-29	Shen Hao (main)	CN	Detention
		Luo Guanghui (supporting)	CN	Detention
		Zhou Bin (supporting)	CN	Detention
		Wang Zhuoming (supporting)	CN	Detention
		Liu Dong (supporting)	CN	Detention
24	2014-11-21	Shen Hao (main)	CN	Arrest
		Liu Dong (supporting)	CN	Arrest
		Chen Dongyang (supporting)	CN	Arrest
		Le Bing (supporting)	CN	Arrest
25	2015-06-22	Zhai Yanmin (main)	CN	Detention
		Liu Jianjun (main)	CN	Detention
		Li Mouli (supporting)	CN	
		Li Mouxiang (supporting)	CN	
26	2015-07-12	Zhou Shifeng, Wu Gan, Liu Sixin, Zhao Wei (main) (all offscreen)	CN	RSDL

Database of forced TV confessions events

		Zhai Yanmin (supporting)	CN	RSDL
		Liu Xing (supporting)	CN	Detention
		Huang Liqun (supporting)	CN	RSDL
27	2015-07-19	**Zhou Shifeng (main), Wang Yu, Wu Gan (offscreen)**	**CN**	**RSDL**
		Liu Sixin (supporting)	CN	RSDL
		Huang Liqun (supporting)	CN	RSDL
		Xie Yuandong (supporting)	CN	RSDL
		Liu Jianjun (supporting)	CN	Detention
		Liu Xing (supporting)	CN	Detention
		Ms Gou (supporting)	CN	
		Ning Huirong (supporting)	CN	
		Zheng Yuming (supporting)	CN	
		(supporting)		RSDL
28	2015-07-19	**Tursan (main)**	**CN (UI)**	
29	2015-07-20	**Ai Ke Abai Er (main)**	**CN (UI)**	
30	2015-08-31	**Wang Xiaolu (main)**	**CN**	**RSDL**
31	2015-10-17	**Wang Yu (main)**	**CN**	**RSDL**
		Bao Longjun (supporting)	CN	RSDL
32	2015-11-26	**Jiang Yefei (main)**	**CN**	Detention
		Dong Guanping (supporting)	CN	Detention
33	2016-01-18	**Gui Minhai (main)**	**SWE**	**Detention or RSDL**
34	2016-01-19	**Peter Dahlin (main)**	**SWE**	**RSDL**

		Wang Qiushi (supporting)	CN	RSDL
		Xing Jianshen (supporting)	CN	RSDL
35	2016-02-01	Ding Ning (main)	CN	Arrested
36	2016-02-25	Zhang Kai (main)	CN	RSDL
		Liu Peng (supporting)	CN	RSDL
37	2016-02-28	Gui Minhai (main)	SWE	*Likely* RS
		Zhang Zhiping (supporting)	HK	*Likely* RSDL
		Lu Bo (supporting)	HK	*Likely* RSDL
38	2016-04-15	Taiwanese telecom fraud (main)	TW	-
		Mr Jian (supporting)	TW	
		Mr Xu (supporting)	TW	
39	2016-05-02	Taiwanese telecom fraud (main)	TW	-
		Mr Lun (supporting)	TW	
		Mr Xu (supporting)	TW	
40	2016-05-17	Xu Qin (main)	CN	Detention or Arrest
41	2016-06-21	Lin Zuluan (main)	CN	Detention or Arrest
42	2016-07-06	Lam Wing-kee (main)	HK	Bail
43	2016-08-01	Wang Yu (main)	CN	Bail
44	2017-03-02	Jiang Tianyong (main)	CN	RSDL

		Xie Yang (supporting)	CN	Arrest

45	**2017-05-09**	**Xie Yang (main)**	**CN**	**Arrest**

46	**2018-02-09**	**Gui Minhai (main)**	**SWE**	**Detention**

47	**2018-04-23**	**Guo Wengui (off-screen)**	**CN**	**Arrest (in absence)**
		Chen Zhiheng (supporting)	CAN	Arrest
		Chen Zhiyu (supporting)	CAN	Arrest

48	**2018-08-17**	**Chen Jieren (main)**	**CN**	**RSDL or Arrest**
		Chen Minren (supporting)	CN	RSDL or Arrest
		Chen Weiren (supporting)	CN	RSDL or Arrest
		Ms Liu (supporting)	CN	RSDL or Arrest

TRIAL BY MEDIA
China's new show trials, and the global expansion of Chinese media

END NOTES

Chapter 1 | INTRODUCTION

[1] *Xin jing bao*, March 2, 2016 http://epaper.bjnews.com.cn/html/2016-03/02/content_624607.htm
[2] Fiskesjö, Magnus, Confessions Made in China: Made in China Journal, Vol 3, Issue 1, Jan-Mar 2018, Pp 18-22, ISSN 2206-9119 (http://www.chinoiresie.info/confessions-made-in-china/)
[3] Fiskesjö, Magnus, The Return of the Show Trial: China's Televised "Confessions: The Asia-Pacific Journal, Vol 15, Issue 13, Number 1, July 2017. (https://apjjf.org/2017/13/Fiskesjo.html)

Chapter 6 | WANG YU

[1] From interview with Epoch Times (http://www.epochtimes.com/gb/18/5/28/n10434103.htm), translated into English and published by ChinaChange (https://chinachange.org/2018/07/01/709-crackdown-three-years-on-mother-and-lawyer-reveals-brutality-against-her-teenage-son-for-the-first-time/) (slightly edited for clarity and brevity)

Chapter 10 | FORCED TV CONFESSIONS

[1] https://supchina.com/2018/08/22/xinjiang-explainer-chinas-reeducation-camps-for-a-million-muslims/
[2] http://www.chinafile.com/document-9-chinafile-translation
[3] https://www.buzzfeed.com/markdistefano/chinas-state-tv-wants-to-hire-a-huge-number-of-journalists?utm_term=.wgbMpM0NY#.qcJ3B3maQ
and https://www.theglobeandmail.com/news/world/uyghurs-around-the-world-feel-new-pressure-as-china-increases-its-focus-on-thoseabroad/article36759591/
[4] Gardner, D. 2017. "Trial by TV: Why is China broadcasting televised confessions of suspects. [Unpublished master's thesis]. National Chengchi University, Taiwan.

Chapter 11 | WEAPONIZED MEDIA, AND RESPONSING TO CHINA'S INFLUENCING OPERATIONS

[1] Chinese Media 'Going Out' in Spanish Speaking Countries: The Case of CGTN-Español https://www.westminsterpapers.org/articles/10.16997/wpcc.277/
[2] https://www.smh.com.au/national/chinese-language-newspapers-in-australia-beijing-controlsmessaging-propaganda-in-press-20160610-gpg0s3.html

[3] https://www.ft.com/content/f5d00a86-3296-11e8-b5bf-23cb17fd1498

[4] Formalizing decisions related to the State taken at the preceding 19th Party Congress in October 2017

[5] From Xi Jinping speech. https://www.ft.com/content/fb2b3934-b004-11e7-beba-5521c713abf4

[6] https://www.theguardian.com/world/2016/feb/19/xi-jinping-tours-chinas-top-state-media-outlets-to-boost-loyalty

[7] Section 11 of the *program for the Deepening Reform of Party and Government Organs* (深化党和国家机构改革方案) http://chinamediaproject.org/2018/03/22/when-reform-means-tighter-controls/

[8] Section 12 of the *program for the Deepening Reform of Party and Government Organs* (深化党和国家机构改革方案) http://chinamediaproject.org/2018/03/22/when-reform-means-tighter-controls/

[9] *program for the Deepening Reform of Party and Government Organs* (深化党和国家机构改革方案) http://chinamediaproject.org/2018/03/22/when-reform-means-tighter-controls/

[10] Section 35 of the *program for the Deepening Reform of Party and Government Organs* (深化党和国家机构改革方案) http://chinamediaproject.org/2018/03/22/when-reform-means-tighter-controls/

[11] Section 36 of the *program for the Deepening Reform of Party and Government Organs* (深化党和国家机构改革方案) http://chinamediaproject.org/2018/03/22/when-reform-means-tighter-controls/

[12] Section 36 of the *program for the Deepening Reform of Party and Government Organs* (深化党和国家机构改革方案) http://chinamediaproject.org/2018/03/22/when-reform-means-tighter-controls/

[13] https://www.nytimes.com/2018/03/21/world/asia/china-communist-party-xi-jinping.html

[14] https://www.uscc.gov/Research/china%E2%80%99s-overseas-united-front-work-background-and-implications-united-states

[15] Magic Weapons: China's political influence activities under Xi Jinping. Brady, Anne-Marie https://www.wilsoncenter.org/article/magic-weapons-chinas-political-influence-activities-under-xi-jinping

[16] https://thediplomat.com/2018/02/chinas-united-front-work-propaganda-as-policy/

[17] https://www.ft.com/content/fb2b3934-b004-11e7-beba-5521c713abf4

[18] Magic Weapons: China's political influence activities under Xi Jinping. Brady, Anne-Marie https://www.wilsoncenter.org/article/magic-weapons-chinas-political-influence-activities-under-xi-jinping

[19] https://supchina.com/2018/10/02/why-state-media-fail-to-make-china-look-good/

[20] https://foreignpolicy.com/2018/10/01/chinas-global-propaganda-is-aimed-at-bosses-not-foreigners/

[21] https://www.hongkongfp.com/2018/10/02/reporter-accused-assault-released-without-charge-diplomatic-pressure-says-chinese-state-tv/

[22] https://www.westminsterpapers.org/33/volume/13/issue/1/

TRIAL BY MEDIA
China's new show trials, and the global expansion of Chinese media

[23] Could Chinese News Channels Have a Future in Latin America?
https://www.westminsterpapers.org/articles/10.16997/wpcc.276/
[24] Chinese Media 'Going Out' in Spanish Speaking Countries: The Case of CGTN-Español https://www.westminsterpapers.org/articles/10.16997/wpcc.277/
[25] Localisation between Negotiating Forces: A Case Study of a Chinese Radio Station in the United States https://www.westminsterpapers.org/articles/10.16997/wpcc.273/
[26] http://africachinareporting.co.za/2017/11/do-africans-trust-chinese-media-opinion-piece/
[27] https://www.ft.com/content/fb2b3934-b004-11e7-beba-5521c713abf4
[28] https://www.ft.com/content/fb2b3934-b004-11e7-beba-5521c713abf4
[29] https://www.ft.com/content/fb2b3934-b004-11e7-beba-5521c713abf4
[30] https://www.ft.com/content/f5d00a86-3296-11e8-b5bf-23cb17fd1498
[31] https://www.smh.com.au/national/chinese-language-newspapers-in-australia-beijing-controlsmessaging-propaganda-in-press-20160610-gpg0s3.html.
[32] https://www.smh.com.au/national/chinese-language-newspapers-in-australia-beijing-controls-messaging-propaganda-in-press-20160610-gpg0s3.html
[33] https://www.ft.com/content/f5d00a86-3296-11e8-b5bf-23cb17fd1498
[34] https://www.lowyinstitute.org/the-interpreter/australian-media-deals-are-victory-chinese-propaganda
[35] https://foreignpolicy.com/2018/09/14/china-is-buying-african-medias-silence/amp/?__twitter_impression=true
[36] http://www.politicsweb.co.za/news-and-analysis/how-independent-is-independent-media
[37] Interview, 2018-10-02
[38] Austria (1), EU (other) (2), France (5), Germany (1), Greece (1), Hungary (6), Ireland (2), Italy (6), Netherlands (1), Portugal (3), Romania (2), Russia (3), Spain (4), Sweden (3), United Kingdom (4).
[39] https://www.smh.com.au/national/chinese-language-newspapers-in-australia-beijing-controls-messaging-propaganda-in-press-20160610-gpg0s3.html
[40] Hard Edge of Sharp Power – Understanding China's influence operations abroad. J. Michael Cole. October 2019, MacDonald-Laurier Institute Publication.
[41] https://www.nzherald.co.nz/nz/news/article.cfm?c_id=1&objectid=11163835
[42] Magic Weapons: China's political influence activities under Xi Jinping. Brady, Anne-Marie https://www.wilsoncenter.org/article/magic-weapons-chinas-political-influence-activities-under-xi-jinping
[43] https://www.ft.com/content/4c23258a-de28-11e7-a8a4-0a1e63a52f9c
[44] https://www.ft.com/content/d3ac306a-e188-11e7-8f9f-de1c2175f5ce
[45] https://www.ft.com/content/fb2b3934-b004-11e7-beba-5521c713abf4
[46] https://www.theguardian.com/world/2018/may/28/new-zealands-five-eyes-membership-called-into-question-over-china-links
[47] https://foreignpolicy.com/2018/09/14/china-is-buying-african-medias-silence/amp/?__twitter_impression=true
[48] https://foreignpolicy.com/2018/09/14/china-is-buying-african-medias-silence/amp/?__twitter_impression=true

TRIAL BY MEDIA
China's new show trials, and the global expansion of Chinese media

---

[49] https://www.nytimes.com/2017/12/11/world/asia/china-germany-linkedin.html
[50] https://www.economist.com/china/2018/06/14/china-is-spending-billions-on-its-foreign-language-media
[51] https://www.bloomberg.com/graphics/2018-china-business-in-europe/
[52] https://www.ft.com/content/f5d00a86-3296-11e8-b5bf-23cb17fd1498
[53] Benner, Thorsten, Jan Gaspers, Mareike Ohlberg, Lucrezia Poggetti and Kristin Shi-Kupfer. Authoritarian Advance: Responding to China's growing political influence in Europe, Global Public Policy Institute and Mercator Institute for China Studies, February. https://www.merics.org/sites/default/fles/2018-02/GPPi_MERICS_Authoritarian_Advance_2018_1.pdf

www.ingramcontent.com/pod-product-compliance
Lightning Source LLC
Chambersburg PA
CBHW031957190326
41520CB00007B/280